EXPAND YOUR BRAND

How to Supersize Any Brand Anywhere in the World

MERRILL PEREYRA

© 2011, Merrill Pereyra

Published by The Messenger Group Pty Ltd
PO Box H241
Australia Square NSW 1215

A CIP catalogue of this book is available from the National Library of Australia.

Pereyra, Merrill

Expand Your Brand

ISBN 978-0-9775519-8-9

The Messenger Group
Editor: Paul C Pritchard
Copy Editor: Linda Vergnani
Cover Design: Luke Gover
Design: Dane Gartrell
www.themessengergroup.com.au

Printed in China

ACKNOWLEDGEMENTS

In my 23 years of employment at McDonald's I am quite certain that I have liaised with, met and been inspired by literally thousands of people. You are too numerous to mention and too important not to mention. So to all those unnamed colleagues and friends: I thank you.

I have had the privilege to work with outstanding teams in many diverse countries. We were often strangers, flung together in unchartered waters, and we stayed afloat because we were resourceful team players. A dream team is a collection of inspired individuals – each wholeheartedly contributing to the whole.

I give a gentle and warm nod of gratitude to Lisa Ransom, Gary Barber, Leslie Lyndon, Asoka Dissanayake, Kathy Choi, Ravini Perera, Gavin Walker, George Kapanaris, Iain Newton and Nick Rodd.

Guy Russo and Andrew Hipsley were amazing leaders and generous supportive mentors – I am eternally grateful.

A big thanks to Cherie Kellahan for your humorous and brilliant help and encouragement in the writing of this book.

A deep appreciation for all at Messenger Publishing for their warm encouragement and professionalism in the creating of this book. Special thanks to Lisa Messenger, Claire Cassey and Paul C Pritchard.

~

All profits from the sale of this book will go to the McDonald's Family Room at the Colonial War Memorial Hospital in Suva, Fiji.

Thank you for your support.

I firstly dedicate this book to three people who I wish were here today. They were there when I took my first steps on this amazing journey:

Eric Gladio for simply hiring me.

Charlie Bell for telling me that anything was possible through hard work and dedication.

Craig McElrath for teaching me to make the best of every day that I live on this earth; to live each day like it was my last and to live with no regrets.

My heartfelt dedication to my beautiful loving family: Ann, Dominique and Gabriel, you keep me grounded and keep me believing in myself.

And of course, last but never least, for mum who always believed in me.

EXPAND YOUR BRAND
CONTENTS

CONTENTS

EXPAND YOUR BRAND

FOREWORD

Foreword by Hans Joe Keil, former minister of Trade and Tourism for the Government of Samoa.

It takes a special kind of person to be sincerely liked and respected in equal measure. During his 23 years at McDonald's Merrill was fiercely committed in achieving ambitious business outcomes. Yet his personal style and character were always expressed with kindness, care and consideration. He forged new frontiers for McDonald's and opened the brand for the first time in countries as diverse as Saudi Arabia, Tahiti, Fiji , Samoa, New Caledonia and American Samoa.

The formula for opening a new territory could not be precisely defined and replicated as it was always so culturally specific. Merrill pioneered his own unique methodology and often relied upon a blend of intuition and street smarts as well as necessary conventional business practices. In smaller countries in the Pacific, such as Samoa, there were many big brands who tried and failed. They all missed the key and fundamental principles of understanding and adapting to new cultures. It is of course about making the new culture adapt to the new brand. However, predominately, it is about the new brand being flexible enough to adapt into the new culture with respect and humility.

Big brands or small brands can learn a lot as Merrill recounts his often challenging and often highly amusing experiences. What follows is an entertaining and educational true-life story highlighting the successes earned and the lessons learned during an impeccable 23 year career. Great leaders, as with good friends, prove their worth over time. Merrill has proved that he will always be a class act.

EXPAND YOUR BRAND

INTRODUCTION

I wanted to write a book that was inspirational and educational. Although it would deal predominantly with the serious business of business, I also wanted to make it anecdotal and light.

McDonald's is renowned for its informal and relaxed management style and its open-door policy even at executive levels. I like that style. Business books need to speak to you and not at you. I have tried to take the dry and indigestible business-speak out. Let's face it, my boss was a clown, so how else would I write?

My fundamental role at McDonald's was to take the concept and the brand and then implement the infrastructure into viable new markets, such as Saudi Arabia, Fiji and Samoa. There were so many challenges and obstacles that invariably changed from state to state, city to city and country to country. I learned not only to think on my feet but also to compute at lightning speed.

I think it's no coincidence that Ronald McDonald is a clown. To expand your business you have to learn to speed juggle with a great big smile on your face and at times dig deep into your bag of magic tricks.

I had an amazing 23-year career with one of the greatest brands of the twentieth century. Then the global financial crisis arrived and told Ronald McDonald that to keep him in wigs and gigs there would need to be some cutbacks. As with many of the big companies it's often the big salaries at the top that are the first to be sacrificed.

After 23 devoted years the word *redundancy* was hard to swallow. At the same time, as a consultant, I would give exactly the same business advice – *trim off the fat*. Tough times demand tough measures. I knew the business logic and the business speak but it still shook me to the core. So I did what I do best; I took a deep breath, stood up tall, brushed myself off, gave old Ronald a high five and embraced the next phase of my already colourful life.

Life was giving me another amazing opportunity, asking me to take stock and reassess everything: my life's purpose, new goals and current ambition. In that reassessment I recognised the enormous wealth of knowledge and experience that I had gained in working my way from the bottom to the top.

I also realised that my experience would be of enormous value and inspiration to many individuals and companies. Yes, the world of business is changing and yet the rudiments and foundations remain mostly unchanged. This is what I would like to impart: how to lay the start-up foundations so that a small business can expand into new territories, new cities and new countries.

This book is my way of summarising and wrapping up the last 23 years. You could say I'm gift wrapping those years into a mini roadmap for the next generation of entrepreneurs and business pioneers.

Incidentally, some of you may be curious and wondering why I chose 23 chapters. It might seem like an odd number (I know it actually is an odd number). Well there are a few reasons I settled on 23. Firstly I was born on 23 September. I migrated to Australia on 23 March 1987 when I was 23 years old. My daughter was born on 23 November and my son on 23 October and coincidently, I was employed by McDonald's for 23 years.

These are a string of seemingly unrelated events or at best a string of coincidences. It's up to us to add and subtract meaning. It's up to all of us to create meaning.

This is an indication of how I see the world and myself, both in my personal and my business life. I have created meaning both strategically and creatively as is demonstrated in the following pages.

I trust that you will be able to take the teachings within this book into your life and the life of your business. I hope they augment your confidence so that you can expand your goals, dreams and potential. Mostly I want to expand your smile and your ability to relax into your business. Enjoy!

CHAPTER
1

HEADING IN THE RIGHT DIRECTION?

"I'm a great believer in luck, and I find the harder I work the more of it I have." - Thomas Jefferson

Time, distance and experience naturally alter our perspective. I now have the luxury of looking back at my life; my hopes, my dreams, my uncertain certainties and my often embarrassing naivety. It's like I'm remembering a series of old movies where, of course, I'm always the central character, but the genre, the location and the cast endlessly change.

With hindsight I can join the dots, make connections and see that it was all perfect. I would not change a thing, not even my naïve arrival in Australia.

I believe that each experience, no matter how trivial or mundane it may first appear, is an essential cog in the mechanics of our whole life. When I arrived in Australia I was different, an alien and everything was new. The culture shock was both challenging and exciting. What I didn't realise at that time was that my experience of arriving in a strange new country and culture was the biggest training workshop that I would ever attend.

Life was preparing me for my long career at McDonald's and specifically my particular career path within the company.

It was teaching essential lesson after lesson in what I would need within my future career at McDonald's: the ability to effortlessly land in new cultures; to hit the ground running with flexibility and agility and to have the foresight and the precision to see and name differences whilst working towards equality and standardisation.

The start of this movie is a Bollywood meets Hollywood comedy. I blush a little when I think about my debut into my Australian movie which happened on a heady day on 23 March 1987 (exactly 23 years before I wrote these words). Picture this: the screen image wobbles and dissolves and we move swiftly back in time.

You see a 23-year-old middle class Indian man from Mumbai arriving at Melbourne airport in Australia with a reasonable standard of English and an unreasonable amount of ambition. By way of education he's only got a Diploma in Food Handling and Technology. He's not exactly naïve but he's still a little wet behind the ears.

He's a good-looking young man with a bright smile and an overly enthusiastic disposition. The newcomer is dressed in a soft, pale blue, tailored linen suit and is dapper, no doubt, but has a little too much starch under the collar compared to his Melbournian peers.

He's in good shape and his stride exudes optimism. His oversized luggage is bursting with promise and the remnants of his Indian lower middle-class life. The housekeeper packed the cases with love, whilst the only other hired help sat on them for closing. He left his modest, but somewhat privileged world a little sadder.

Now this young man is trying very hard to glide seamlessly into the new Australian culture, to fit right in mate! And here is where the Indian peg learns all about Australian holes; where one man's difference bumps up against a country of multicultural diversity, the likes of which he has never seen.

Now in 100 countries, Ronald McDonald opens the first Tahiti store.

The first shock is the cold air that grabs him by the throat as he disembarks from the aeroplane. Then he makes the natural assumption that it must be a national holiday or much worse; a national day of mourning. Why else is there no porter to carry his bags off the carousel?

His sister and her family greet him at the airport and then they all pile into a car that his sister's husband actually drives himself. There is no driver. Somebody very important must have died for all the staff to be given a day off.

He arrives at his sister's modest suburban home and is shown around. He is surprised a few hours later when he returns to his room to find his bags are exactly where he left them and they are still unpacked. Where is the housekeeper? In 1987 in India it cost less than 10 cents to have all your bags carried and a housekeeper was paid $30 a month. All this is now a world away and so begins his integration into a new way of life: self-service Australia.

His father had died from cancer when he was only two years old. So he was raised by his mum, his three older sisters and the compulsory league of well-intentioned aunties. All their advice and grooming is mostly useless right now in this alien culture.

However, he remembers, with a sting, one remark an uncle had made to his mother that this boy would never amount to anything much. This pivotal moment pierced him then and stings him now. But it's also like rocket fuel for his determination to make it in the world. It's another almost invisible but vital cog in his future success story.

Determined, he unpacks his own bags and puts on his tailored suit and handmade cotton shirt and heads out to downtown Bourke Street. In true Mr Bean style he obeys the red man flashing at the crossing. He stops exactly where he is – right on the tram tracks with a tram careering towards him. A true-blue Aussie saves him in the nick of time by grabbing his hand.

Our young hero is shocked at this direct display of intimacy and pleads, 'Let go of my hand man – what are you doing?' The man pulls him out of the way and glares at our confused hero. 'Struth mate, ya nearly carked it and ruined me arvo.'

Opening day Suva, Fiji Islands.

(Standard English translation: 'I say old chap, you almost got yourself killed and that would have inconvenienced me for the whole afternoon.')

And right there is the biggest shock of all: Australians do not speak English; they speak a strange and colourful dialect called Aussie.

Undeterred and in a desperate bid to assimilate into the culture and stay away from the pavements he does what any young man with drive would do. He looks for something with magnetism to drive. His hormones and peer pressure get the better of him and he buys an old, bright yellow Holden Monaro - the colour of a lemon. Oblivious to the cultural stigma attached to such a vehicle, he drives to his first interview at McDonald's CBD.

He makes an easy mistake and goes to the McDonald's in Bourke Street Mall - which is for pedestrian use only. He drives there. No, I mean he literally drives there, through the mall and parks right outside. People are waving and jeering and telling him he can't drive into the mall and park. You must remember that he's still in between two worlds, India and Australia. He's not going to move his new car for anyone.

Inside, the manager explains that his interview is meant to be at the other McDonald's. So he drives out of the mall and arrives at his interview on time. The interview goes well and he is gainfully employed. And so begins his 23 years at McDonald's. (Incidentally, he takes the credit for the huge concrete bollards that went up around all Australian malls and shopping precincts after that fateful day.)

So, what has all this got to do with business? It's simple. Without realising it the culture difference and culture shock was educating me into the art of cultural diversity. I was being groomed by my everyday experience. Unique core competencies were being instilled within me. I needed bounce-back resilience and an ability to laugh and move on, even if the joke was on me.

My personality was being shaped for bigger business. This is still something I look for in new and in particular, young staff. What is their individual journey equipping them for? How are their strengths, challenges and talents expressed? In remapping my own follies and triumphs, identifying my own skill sets and skill gaps, I could better help employ and manage theirs.

The one thing that immediately impressed me about McDonald's was that 'the sky was the limit'; promotion and career advancement were performance based. The training was world-class and I was encouraged to constantly upgrade my skills. There was a clear career path mapped out with specific targets and requirements that would take you straight to the top. If you were conscientious, showed initiative and had a brain ... it was a no brainer!

The one thing that immediately impressed me about McDonald's was that 'the sky was the limit'; promotion and career advancement were performance based.

McDonald's was a burgeoning global franchise enterprise. This was a company that was geared to rewarding its high performing employees, regardless of their race, education and background. I worked hard, I was flexible and I said YES a lot. We were a perfect match!

Key Points

- Businesses are run by teams of individuals. Seeing employees as individuals will strengthen your team.

- Look for innate intelligence within yourself and your employees and remember that intelligence does not always come with a degree or a diploma.

- Identify career paths for yourself, your employees and your business. Do you know where you want to be in three, five or ten years?

- Take calculated risks with keen vigilance. You either win or you learn from your mistake. But you have to stay alert!

- Be flexible – mentally, physically, geographically – follow-up on all opportunities. Again: be vigilant in networking and opportunity.

- Ask the opinions of the new kids on the block. Sometimes they see more and can give new and different perspectives. They'll often surprise you!

- Take everything life throws at you as a positive learning experience.

- Your biggest assets are determination, drive and ambition.

- Be ready for anything, smile and say YES.

Lead by pristine example. Let your eminent standards shine and be reflected back to you by your team.

CHAPTER

2

IS IT FEASIBLE?

I am now going to use one of the most important words in business. Most people give it a cursory glance when they should be writing it on a post-it note and sticking it on their foreheads. The word is *feasibility*.

McDonald's is often referred to as, the 'most successful small business in the world'. It started in California in 1940 when Dick and Mac McDonald opened McDonald's Bar-B-Que restaurant. By 1948 it had reinvented itself to look and feel more like the McDonald's that we know today. In 1949 they introduced french-fries and it all ticked along nicely.

It wasn't until 1954 when a salesman named Ray Kroc visited the store that everything really changed. Kroc imagined a franchisee chain of stores all over America. His concept-philosophy was based on the simple principle of a three-legged stool: one leg was McDonald's, the second, the franchisee, and the third, McDonald's suppliers. You can only sit on a stool with a minimum of three legs.

The first of the distinctive restaurants, designed by architect Stanley Meston had opened in Phoenix the previous year. It had the strong red colours and the now famous bright yellow golden arches. First day sales were $366.12. By 1965 there would be over 700 identical restaurants throughout the United States.

No other brand exploded on the world stage, faster and more successfully than McDonald's. It's a multi-billion dollar enterprise that continues to evolve. By February 2011 there were more than 32,500 restaurants in around 117 countries. At one time McDonald's was opening a restaurant somewhere in the world every four hours.

This is how I saw my job setting up the Pacific.

How is that a 'small' business? Simple – each store is run like a small family business. And they are all run like clockwork. This does not mean that every city or country is ripe for a McDonald's. The question that should be on every pioneer's lips: *Is it feasible?*

Everybody wants a picture with Ronald McDonald.

Feasibility is the cornerstone of every business. And throughout the following chapters we will be exploring this concept in various guises. The business has to be feasible and so does your commitment and alignment to your personal goals and vision.

Ray Kroc did not invent the Hamburger but he's known for putting it on the assembly line. And when he realised that his vision and aspirations did not match those of the McDonald brothers, he acted quickly. The McDonald brothers were happy to tick along with their hometown ways. They did not want more risks and more disruption in their contented lives.

But Ray Kroc wanted to make McDonald's the biggest and the best. He believed so much in his vision and the feasibility of it that he bought the McDonald brothers out and never looked back.

Key Points

- Align your personal vision and goals with that of your business.

- Be on the same page as your partner(s) or close the book.

- Have the word feasibility woven into your business plan without allowing vision, dreaming and creativity to be strangled.

- Ask the question: Are you an entrepreneur, who enjoys taking risks or do you prefer a steadier more conservative approach? Nothing wrong with either – just get clear about which one you are!

- Devote serious time to know who you are and who you are not. And in the immortal words of Shakespeare; *'To thine own self be true'.*

Be on the same page as your partner(s) or close the book.

CHAPTER

3

WAIT OR POUNCE?

There are often so many mixed messages around business. We are told to be aggressive, strike while the iron is hot, be competitive, ruthless and spontaneous and vigorously taught that the early bird catches the worm. And at the same time we are instructed about business planning, forecasts, due-diligence, market research, test pilots, prediction trends etc.

It's a fine art and it takes honed business acumen to simultaneously walk both these tightropes. In many ways it cannot be taught. As the world and the market changes so too does the way in which we do business. So one blueprint for all decades will not work.

The fine art of business is primarily gained by two means. One you can practice and the other you attain over time. Respectively, the first is awareness. The second is direct experience – and that includes the successes and the failures.

I cannot emphasise enough how expanding your business awareness will undoubtedly make you a better businessperson. You will be more discerning and absolutely sure when to wait and when to pounce. Awareness is the tiger's best friend. Not speed, or teeth or muscle but knowing when to engage those attributes in the exact perfect moment.

Stealth breeds wealth.

Subliminally the tiger is asking: 'Is this the perfect moment to pounce?'

When I went into a prospective new area my subliminal feasibility radar was permanently activated. I became focused on the task at hand. Relating everything back to the fundamental question of feasibility. One of the most amazing things about moving into a new country or territory is that everything you do is so different from one area to the next. There's never a dull moment.

I would say to my team, 'The devil makes work for idle hands and God rewards those who clean, are punctual and flip a mean burger!' Although each new prospective area is unique, they will all have to subscribe to common basic feasibility law. These common observations become the easy targets, the easily identifiable must haves on your fast checklist, for example: power, water, infrastructure, accessibility, manpower, local suppliers and a prospective market. It seems obvious and it is.

> The devil makes work for idle hands and God rewards those who clean, are punctual and flip a mean burger!

I suggest looking at the three main aspects that influence feasibility:

1. **Financial Feasibility** – often a clear yes or no. For example, a feasibility study in Papua New Guinea came out as 70 per cent positive. This looked good enough on paper but we felt the risk was too great and therefore we

did not go ahead. We also realised that because of the local economy, we could not rely solely on sales from the locals and we could not count on expats alone. You also need to be realistic about when you tip over into profit. It will vary for every business but it can often take between two and three years.

2. **Personal Feasibility** – Do I have what it takes? Is my heart in it? Do I have the level of commitment and stamina required? Can I give this amount of time without impinging on my other responsibilities? Really look at your own goals and motivation. Be honest about your stamina and long-term vision.

3. **Ego Feasibility** – This is where I look for blind spots. I ask a colleague to play devil's advocate; to try and trip me up, to see if there is anything that I am not seeing because I want it so bad. It might be that if it pays off I get a huge promotion or if it works I get the big bonus or maybe just kudos from my peers. We are all human and all susceptible to this. It takes a mature businessperson to investigate these possible blind spots.

Key Points

- Make business your business.

- Activate your feasibility awareness radar and keep it switched on!

- Right timing is essential. Know when to strike like a tiger and when to hold back.

- Get a clear estimation on timings and figures for return on investments.

- Be transparent and conservative about your expectations, especially if you have joint venture partners or other key stakeholders.

- Make sure that you are always on the same page with your partners.

- Check that your desire and emotional attachments are well and truly separated from the financial feasibility.

Marc McElrath (centre), partner for Fiji.

CHAPTER

4

CAN I HAVE SPIES WITH THAT?

FEASIBILITY UNDERCOVER

Once all the basic boxes are ticked the real undercover work gets underway. Taking a brand into a new terrain forces you to find the best route in and discover what lies behind the tourist facade. Before building a business in unfamiliar territory, inspect the site thoroughly and dig down to find if there is bedrock on which you can build sound foundations.

What better way to start any 'new' business or new aspect of your business than at the very beginning! That's right – get out your business plan and dust off the cobwebs. If you don't have a business plan then you need to get working on one right away. It's the blueprint for your business. It should be fun and a very rewarding creative process. Sure there are the necessary SWOT analysis (strengths, weaknesses, opportunities and threats). You need to consider the statistics and forecasts, the cash-flow and spreadsheets, the sustainability and possibility. The there are the number crunching, tax boggling, mine-fields to tackle, but even that can be fun. It's about dreaming big and flying high with an anchor firmly in your business plan.

One of the most important functions of your business plan is to illuminate profit and loss. Profit is the bottom line of any business. With this forever-changing document in your briefcase or on your laptop your mission is not impossible. Undercover Feasibility is the name of your assignment.

Okay, so it's not as dangerous or perhaps as glamorous as movie espionage but I did fancy myself as a kind of spy. I was always on a reconnaissance mission of sorts. Sure, I learned quickly that being Mac Bond was bloody hard work and I often fell into bed exhausted without a bond girl such as Ursula Andress.

The main things a feasibility spy needs are: something to write on, intuition (not often mentioned in business but sometimes your gut feeling is all you have), and most importantly a smile. I found it best to come into new areas, especially new countries, in as low-key a manner as possible.

Be careful when you are making your hotel bookings. I was travelling to Vietnam to do a feasibility study and my secretary had booked the hotel under the company name. So when we arrived the hotel had a banner outside welcoming McDonald's to the country. It totally blew my cover!

I always prefer grassroots feasibility studies. Literally walking the streets, counting the passing cars at crucial intersections, monitoring the busiest shopping districts, just observing everything that might be a clue. If the streets are busy, it's important to know why. Is your competition near? How good is the competition?

I did this in the Pacific region and it paid off. I literally counted the cars that would go through the busiest intersection in a 15-minute block. I ate in the local cafés and watched the local people, studied menus and pricing.

If we were taking the McDonald's brand into virgin territory we obviously could not use the Big Mac Index [1]. So I invented my own – The Mac Bond Index. I would buy bread, milk, flour, butter, eggs and a couple of canned drinks. I would then buy the same items in Sydney and other cities to get an idea of the local economy and monetary value.

And at the end of a gruelling day when I was just about to kick back and phone Ursula or another Bond beauty, I'd remember my secret after dark mission. I would always be curious about the evening business trading activities. You have to think about trading hours immediately. Being open for business is your business. When do the public most want and need your service or product?

It sounds simple, but simplicity in the early stages fans out to efficiency in the later stages. In Samoa, there was little night-time or Sunday trading and McDonald's set trends and awakened many sleepy districts, thus stimulating the economy.

MAC BOND TIP

If you have an established competitor find out as much as you can both discreetly and ethically. You do not want to tread on any toes, especially at this early stage. Get smart about the information you need. For example, I would go into other fast-food outlets in the morning, lunchtime and dinnertime. I would go to the same cash register and the docket would tell me the order number – I could get an idea of how many orders were being processed in a day.

Whilst at the cafes always take time to read the local newspaper. You can glean an enormous amount of information about the political, social, and business climate. The social and political mood of a region or new country is vital information. Spreadsheets and number crunching is only useful when it is paired with real life and real consumers.

Another strategy I used was to make contact with the key accounting and legal firms as well as banks. Business today still thrives on nepotistic, symbiotic relationships. Most of these firms were happy to court my acquaintance, in the hope that if we were to establish a franchise in their area then they would get my patronage.

Tahiti Crew at the product launch of Breakfast.

I would gain public information (so no legal concerns) about who had the money and which businesses were producing it. In a franchise-based business this can be essential. Who do

Expand Your Brand

you want to align with? It's not enough to know **who's who** anymore but also **who's connected to who** and **how**. Finding this out is far more useful.

Another great source of valuable information are expats. They have already come in as the new kids on the block and they now know the ropes and the hidden threats, and perhaps more importantly they know the hidden potential.

Usually in a smaller territory or country you will sooner or later be discovered. Here is where the art of diplomacy comes in: knowing what to say and when. Disclose only what is essential, not too little, not too much, but just enough.

Occasionally governments contacted me. I never declined a meeting and simply explained what I was doing, stressing that this was a reconnaissance mission only. Nothing was set in stone.

At this early stage your mission is to unearth the dirt as well as the diamonds. Apply this philosophy to new suburbs as well as new cities and new countries. Anticipate every eventuality and record all findings and observations in your business plan.

Key Points

- Explore new territory quietly. You can raise your profile later.

- Every business needs different start-up information. Get curious about the information that is specific to your business. It can be a lot of fun.

- Hypothetical should be your middle name.

- Competitor comparison will save your bacon!

- Get into the local economy, mindset and politics of your new customers.

- Remember it's the locals who will sustain your business and tourism and transients will boost sales. But serve the locals first!

- Learn to say not too much, not too little – but just enough!

- Leave no stone unturned.

- It's better to spend some money on a strong feasibility study and decide not to move forward than to spend a fortune trying to float a flagship with 13 holes in its side.

> Remember it's the locals who will sustain your business and tourism and transients will boost sales. But serve the locals first!

- To be forewarned is to be forearmed, so prepare.

[1] The Big Mac Index is an informal system that compares and measures the purchasing power between currencies. For example, one Australian Dollar might equal one US dollar. But it might take US$3 and AU$4 to buy a big Mac and small fries. It crudely shows how far a currency will stretch.

CHAPTER
5

THINK GLOBALLY, ACT LOCALLY

One of the things that I drove home to my team was to understand and embody the concept of thinking globally whilst acting and thinking like a local.

It was vital to really understand how the brand worked globally and then fine-tune, hone and tailor it for a specific and local market. Even huge brands, like McDonald's, that appear to have a clone-like roll out are all subtly different.

Use your brain; think about it - it makes great emotional sense.

When consumers feel that they are being independently catered for, even in subtle ways, there is an effortless increase in their loyalty to your brand.

It's important to look at the local life-style and spending power. If we look at affordability, for example, in Australia an employee would have to work less than an hour to be able to afford a burger, fries and drink, while in Fiji or Samoa an employee would have to work a lot more hours to be able to afford the same meal.

Going into a new country we would look at ways to balance the needs and often bottom-line demands of the global business with the needs of the new local restaurant. It's a fine balance and the initial set-up is crucial.

Ronald in Tahiti.

BIG FISH SMALL PONDS

The initiatives and creative possibilities are endless. The strategic planning and co-ordination of business and marketing activities can play a major part in boosting your business profile and presence. McDonald's has partnered with FIFA World Cup and The Olympics and how that impacts a local smaller country or enterprise can be very exciting and profitable.

It's a great idea to localise the marketing and get the staff involved. In Samoa we had some of the staff carry the Olympic torch. This was an amazing experience for so many people – for them it was like hitting the jackpot. This sort of energy has a positive ripple effect throughout your consumer community. You might also ask local soccer players or Olympic competitors to become involved in your marketing or advertising campaigns. Local celebrity is as big as global celebrity in smaller districts. The local big fish can boost sales just as well as the global big fish.

ACCLIMATISE

Your feasibility studies must include the merging of the local and the global trends. Always ask will your brand fit in? And how can we make a better fit? Just a little local flavour can significantly boost sales. Look at some of the things you can do to make sure your global brand or national brand fits into the local culture.

Taro is a sweet, edible tuber that is the Pacific islanders' equivalent of a potato. In American Samoa, this vegetable is cheap and more readily available than many fruits. So, we made the supplier in the United States come up with a taro pie, similar to the apple pie, and it was a huge seller. The locals were familiar with the vegetable; they felt personally catered for; they trusted us and repaid us with customer loyalty.

Try and add something local to the menu and also honour local religious values. In Fiji we ensured and advertised that we were Halal Certified. Without this cultural knowledge the store would have lost 20 to 30 per cent of customers. Intense and in-depth feasibility studies will reveal all the nuances that you can easily overlook. An adaptable business is a sustainable business.

Even the smallest of gestures towards local cultural awareness can make a big difference. In Tahiti we served French fries with mayonnaise instead of ketchup as this is how the locals eat their fries.

Business trends are as important as cultural trends, including food trends. If a similar brand has moved into new areas or countries with fundamentally different cultures, try and learn from their experience. What were the barriers and what were the solutions?

I would insist that my teams were engaged in business trends, both local and international. The business world is just like a spider's web. A break in the web in Wall Street can have a ripple effect in Samoa. Just being plugged in and genuinely interested in the fascinating world of local and international business can give you that competitive edge. If you have no interest in business then maybe you are in the wrong business.

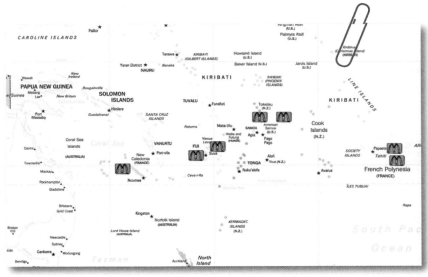

Map of the South Pacific.

Expand Your Brand

In-flight magazine on Air Pacific.

In your research, look at the last five years, even the last ten or twenty years of your new destination. In this digital age even the smallest territories can usually show growth trends and statistics for population, export, import, inflation, new businesses, closed businesses, property sales, properties built, etc. Keeping abreast of the most significant business trends in a new territory will help you assimilate into a culture and make the right choices.

The Internet is an instant information source and now with subscriptions, bloggers and Tweeters there is no excuse to not have your finger on the pulse. Sign up for global business development, investment opportunity and banking newsletters. Explore trends and research information from sites such as, local and federal government departments, industry groups, trade organisations and consulting groups. You will quickly learn to scan what is relevant to you.

Encourage team discussions and forums. When the team members are involved and connected they will feel they can make an impact. Their spontaneous and constructive participation will bring greater job satisfaction. It's a great way to see who has a natural aptitude for business and to sort out the workers from the leaders. It keeps your brain strong and you can network with the best of them!

Remember your staple income is from the local consumers and the transients are the icing on the cake. It's simple: No cake ... then nothing to put the icing on!

Having a flexible plan for the next year, two years and five years will be your anchor. It's better to be over cautious. Remember your staple income is from the local consumers and the transients are the icing on the cake. It's simple: No cake ... then nothing to put the icing on!

You might not always be prepared but you can learn from past surprises. There was a coup in Fiji that was disruptive and often dangerous. Like the rest of the country we navigated through it all and ensured that we had a system in place if something like that were ever to happen again.

In looking at the political climate it's important to remain as objective as possible. If you are thinking about moving into an area that is unwaveringly at odds with your own cultural values and political slant – then maybe think again. Look at local and national politics and understand the basic terrain. Do not side with any one party. Stay neutral. Then you are friends with whichever party is elected. This is important in volatile or highly politicised countries.

In writing this chapter I think I need to emphasise that all of this serious business can be great fun. It's intriguing detective work and the end result is more money with less effort.

Key Points

- Put yourself in the customers' shoes. Locals provide your staple income.

- Think about emotional impacts as well as spreadsheets.

- Merge the global and the local in marketing and advertising.

- Know your new territory inside out and keep your finger on the pulse.

- Read bloggers, tweeters and subscribe to the world around you.

- Small cultural gestures translate into big sales.

- Make the political climate and the weather your business.

- Get curious, have fun and expand personally and professionally.

- Expect and accept that there will be ups and downs.

- Smile and remember that no matter how bad the situation is there is always a silver lining. No matter what happens today the sun will rise tomorrow.

CHAPTER
6

A MATTER OF VALUES

McDonald's has a very succinct yet broad philosophy about its values. It puts **quality, service, cleanliness and value** first. There is no preferred sequence or order: they all come first. And there is no compromise. Every department lives and breathes these principles and the golden arches empire is built upon them.

Execution is king. If you apply these values rigorously and diligently your business will improve. There will be a natural alignment with integrity and work ethics that can bolster any business at any stage of its development.

If you aspire to have consistent profits then you must be consistent. It's not something that you will do at the end of the day or when you open shop. It has to be second nature; it has to be woven into every second of the day. Instilling this within everyone from executives to front-of-house staff is one of the best uses of your time.

But you have to be authentic. This is the key to my success. I never asked anyone to carry out what I either would not do myself or something that I did not believe in. Trust me, authentic leadership is powerful. Some people might not resonate with you or your beliefs. That's okay too. They just get a chance to see that they are in the wrong industry.

Money lubricates a sweet lifestyle, but if you don't enjoy how you make that money it might land in the bank with all sorts of bitter contracts. Love what you do and your customers too.

Samoa-Apia restaurant.

I often resent tipping someone for *just* doing their job. But when someone enthusiastically offers that little bit more, I tip abundantly. We've all experienced it. We all recognise that certain magical interaction with someone who is really committed to the task at hand and is putting you first without compromising their own life's course. They are not suspicious that you are a secret shopper or part

> Love what you do and your customers too.

of the Undercover Boss TV Crew. We get a sense that they genuinely know what they are doing, why they are doing it and, within their bigger life plan, for how long. They treat people how they want to be treated.

Most successful business will have a regular and effective grading system. Make a transparent plan of when and how each department or store will be graded. Be exact: how many times per year and on what dates. Make the grading system and criteria easy to read and follow for all concerned from crew to executive levels.

Clearly state the procedures necessary to always score well. Ensure that the feeling around the evaluation is around support and augmentation of standards and is not a 'test' for flaws. It should also be an appraisal and acknowledgement of what is working. Having clear values should make the grading, the correction and the disciplinary procedures far easier to execute. Everyone should be working with the same book of great expectations!

Many businesses can use **quality, service, cleanliness and value** as their main pillars, but perhaps yours needs to be different, more specific. Another axiom that I used throughout my career was 'Be specific and your results will be terrific!' I found that the more I worked with specifics and relevant detail the more options I had.

Really think about your business. What does your brand stand for? Can you stand behind it? There might be a whole lot more on your list but what are you going to name as your top four values. What are immoveable? The more you put on your list the clearer you will get about who you want to be and where you want to be.

If you and your business have integrity with your principles and values, then there are four more elements that should effortlessly rush to the front and be counted.

1. Increasing profits

2. Sustainability

3. Job satisfaction

4. More time to delegate and play

The last four elements (also in no particular order) should be the goal-pillars of every business.

Key points

- Identify the values of your business and brand and then live and breathe them.

- Authentic leadership is powerful.

- Model strong work ethics and surround yourself with like-minded people. Ambitious teams can spark healthy, competitive and productive think-tanks.

- Reward hard work as it always pays off. Performance-based promotional paths are highly motivational for high achievers.

- Integrity is essential to your business and leads to increasing profits and job satisfaction.

Reward hard work as it always pays off. Performance-based promotional paths are highly motivational for high achievers.

CHAPTER

7

BUSINESS SUSTAINABILITY

Often things can be achieved or attained, but they are not always sustainable. Sometimes that does not matter. If you can get a sharp enough profit spike for a short shelf life of a product or marketing strategy then it might just be worth it. However, for the most part the implementation of a new product or venture will have a high initial start-up cost. It has to be sustainable long enough to recoup all the initial financial investments and then tip right over into profit. The profit has to have a determined margin. If it's just sitting on the profit line then it may not have been worth all the time, energy, money and planning.

Business is all about risks but a calculated risk is the only risk you should be willing to take. If there is a grey area or especially if the sustainability question leads to more and more questions, you might want to ask the opinion of somebody with more experience: your accountant, bank-manager, marketing manager, a competitor, your kids! Ask anyone for an informed opinion so that you can make and trust your own.

When planning your business strategies and budget always ask the question: **Is it sustainable** and if so, for how long? Make this part of your daily thinking – let it fuse into all aspects of your business. It can apply to almost everything from the purchasing of new equipment, the hiring of new staff to fads or fleeting changes in the market.

The market is of course inexhaustible but it is also both fickle and temperamental. There is a whole science behind customer loyalty that is constantly being upgraded. What worked for one generation might not necessarily work for the next.

Knowing when to implement and more importantly when to withdraw a product or service will save a lot of anxiety down the line. And very often that might be a thin line that you are walking. A thin line between profit and loss or a thin line between stay open or shut up shop. I must reiterate – vigilance is critical in business.

When we opened the first store in Fiji we did not achieve half of the break even sales in the first six months, the site we had was great long-term, but in the short term we needed to have a business that would

> Be bold with risks but not so bold as to be foolish! Do the math before you walk unknown paths.

be positive cash flow in the first twelve months. We decided to move quickly and open the second restaurant in the capital Suva. This store was in the heart of the city and did very well. It helped us to keep the first business afloat whilst courting new customers.

Even something as regular and in-demand as a burger is at the whim of the times, the people and the education of a nation. In 2003 McDonald's added 'premium salads' to its menu. It was time. It was in direct response to the public's demand. It was an intelligent move to offer an alternative to burger and fries. It catered for more people, the whole family. It addressed the problem of obesity sweeping Western nations. In just this small act of offering a healthier choice, McDonald's became part of the fast-food healthier choices revolution. It upgraded its image by upgrading its customer care.

My wife once said to me, 'Oh Honey, I make you do the sweetest things!' Following this logic you can allow the customer to be right and still have it your way.

Fiji Suva store.

Sometimes when your timing is right, it's hard to distinguish who's leading the changes. Is it market pressure and demand or is it business initiative and correct forecasting? The trick is to move with the times or even better stay one step ahead.

Key Points

- Always ask about sustainability and longevity in all areas of your business. You might be surprised where it can apply.

- Shelf life is a key to sustainability, often literally and metaphorically.

- If you are unsure about the sustainability of some aspects of your business then ask an expert – seek out informed opinions!

- Stay flexible and agile: allow room to grow and morph into more profitable and timely income generators.

- Stay one-step ahead or if you can two or more steps ahead.

- If the sales of the business are not meeting break-even, then move to your first backup plan and maybe even to your second.

> If the sales of the business are not meeting break-even, then move to your first backup plan and maybe even to your second.

- Remember that your business sustainability has an impact on environmental sustainability. They should be inextricably linked for positive change.

CHAPTER

8

STRATEGY

O f course the concept of good strategy is woven through this book but I wanted to really bring special attention to it. Knowing what you want and knowing it is possible are two-thirds of the puzzle. How you get there and what strategies you deploy or don't deploy make up the third vital, complex and arbitrary pieces of the puzzle.

Expansion is a constant re-evaluation and re-working of strategies. By their very nature all strategies around expansion must be flexible and updateable. One of the keys to understanding your strategy is to keep a close eye on the market: sometimes consistent and sometimes volatile. Examine the trends and the implications they produce on your sales and demand. Survey and identify the external factors, such as industry trends, your current and new customers' habits, government policies and practices, global and local trends and what impact they may have on your organisation. I did many feasibility studies in countries and would decide against going in if some of these factors were a bigger than usual concern.

- I used to look at currency trends, which are easy to obtain, and if the graph was on a downward trend I might decide against going into a country or at least postpone our entry. I would turn my focus to a more profitable entry that was more favourable for return on investment (ROI) for the bigger McDonald's corporation.

- Another key to this is to understand the labour force issues. In the Pacific, for example, the French unions could be difficult to navigate. Experience was necessary. Sadly sometimes nepotism was involved in employment practices too.

- Find out who your current competitors are as well as who else is planning to come into this new territory – something that is extremely overlooked. Comparisons need to be drawn immediately on brand, service, product and pricing.

Patrick LaFleur (left) partner for New Caledonia.

Remember that one failure in a small country is still seen as a failure for the global parent company. In the McDonald's scenario, all fingers would point to Ronald and not the joint venture partners. So your small enterprise has to also continuously support the global or bigger brand reputation.

It's best to keep strategy simple. Focus on key elements. The ripple effect or flow will also need management further down the track but on a necessity basis. In other words you can cross some bridges when you come to them. Just focus on the bridges that you already know have a toll fee or are dangerous to cross.

Examples of key strategic elements:

- market stability

- financial returns

- labour force and how easily it can be managed

- competition and how the pie will be sliced

- impact on global brand image and reputation.

To ensure that I really knew my strategy inside and out, I would explain it to an esteemed colleague who would be able to play devil's advocate.

WORST CASE SCENARIOS

Plan for the worst scenario that is specific to the country in which you are planning to expand. What are your major threats to your operating hours?

In Fiji and Samoa we had to plan for natural disasters. There are of course cyclones and typhoons, hurricanes, floods and electrical storms. Every store was built to withstand a category 5 cyclone and had reliable and durable back-up power generators. When the storms had passed we could open business immediately and were often the only warm and dry place to get food.

Extreme things happen all the time and in some areas they happen more often. After most disasters McDonald's would always be the first food place to open and often we were able to send food to volunteers and the emergency services.

When a political coup happened in Fiji we were totally unprepared. Yet, quick thinking and fast action saved the business and therefore the livelihood of many, many people. Some of the following improvised tactics became protocol for political and natural disasters.

- Inform all overseas suppliers.

- Increase security.

- Ensure staff are informed and manage their schedules.

- Work out how you can support the community in this time of need. We used to deliver burgers and water to rescue crews in Fiji.

> Get the parent company to step in and help with money or donations to staff who are affected.

- Keep reassuring the staff that all will be okay.

- Get the parent company to step in and help with money or donations to staff who are affected.

- Rearrange your product or service and timelines.

- Be honest with staff and customers – keep them informed. People feel calmer when they know what is going on.

- Never take unnecessary risks.

Olivier Loyant (left) partner for Tahiti, Ravini Perera and myself.

CHAPTER
9

SUPPLY CHAIN BASICS

You are only as good or reliable as your supply chain. Keeping this in mind enables McDonald's to deliver the same product consistently throughout the world. This is quite an achievement and most global businesses marvel at how this is so succinctly achieved.

In very basic terms, most businesses are in the middle of a supply chain. In the restaurant business we need ingredients from trusted suppliers. We turn those supplies into an edible commodity and supply them to the customer. If we stay with the analogy of the food industry, if you have poor ingredients then it stands to reason that you'll have poor food to serve to your customers. If you have varying and unreliable quality from your suppliers you will no doubt have inconsistent taste and quality for your customers. It pretty much works the same with every other business.

Your supply chain needs to be:

- consistent with quality

- reliable

- connected to a strong contingency plan

- competitively priced without compromising on quality.

Once you are established the suppliers will come knocking on your door. But when you are starting out you will need to do extensive and comprehensive research to fine the best supplier match for your needs. Once your orders are consistent and large enough you will have leverage to guarantee orders and therefore drive down the cost. Still, you should aim to get the best price possible as soon as possible. Aim for longevity in your partnerships – think of it as a happy marriage rather than a one-night stand!

Logistics Mapping is concerned with three basic pillars: cost, location and transport.

1. ***COST***
   Find the best price. There are of course variables that might seem at first to make no sense. Logistics may not always appear logical. For example, in New Caledonia we could get products from neighbouring countries Australia or New Zealand but as New Caledonia is a French territory we could get some products from France and the low import taxes would make it favourable to buy from France. Therefore timing and shipment of supply was factored in. As well as import tax, you must follow currency trends if you are purchasing from overseas. Costs can fluctuate dramatically with the rise and fall of currency rates.

2. ***LOCATION***
   Where do your supplies come from? Always look at local produce as it serves the local economy. A stronger local economy has stronger buying power. If the cost were marginal with importing supplies versus local supplies, I would always choose local. It makes good sense in terms of goodwill and self-preservation. The savings on import tax are often what tips the balance. But remember

that import tax is also subject to government regulation and can change yearly or more frequently with volatile governments and economies.

3. **_TRANSPORT_**

    How are supplies transported? Is the transport reliable and how fast can goods get to you? Every supplier will give you their best-case scenario with regards to delivery times but you need to allow for delays and unforeseen events. Local road transport is often more reliable.

Because of the nature of McDonald's and the already world-renowned brand expectation, I would often not take 'local' risks when entering a new country or territory. I have always tried to keep the initial investment and opening costs as low as possible. I would aim for the new venture to have a positive cash flow as soon as possible. In the case of McDonald's a positive cash flow meant that the joint venture partners or investors were happy because early signs of success instil a sense of confidence for the future. It also meant that the corporate leadership teams were positive and therefore more willing to take risks and be patient for sales and profits to increase.

In most cases I would import between 90 to 100 per cent of the products into the country. This of course was calculated and the safest option. After a few months or a year, when I had a good understanding of the trends and the customer count and sales forecasts were more accurate, I would look at how we could have a migration plan to get some of the products locally and at the same time ensure that they met the global quality standards.

I would source a good local bakery that could follow the McDonald's bun recipe to the letter. Lettuce and tomatoes were also easier to source locally and because of their short shelf-life it was better to have them delivered more regularly. Printing and paper stock because of weight was more cost effective locally. I took a great sense of pride in opening avenues for small local businesses and increasing their income stream. A lot of jobs were created in opening a 'local' McDonalds both at the restaurant and the supply chains in its orbit.

Salad launch in Tahiti.

Because the McDonald's standard is so exact it really raised the bar for local enterprises that wanted to supply and work with us. Many local suppliers, with the promise of huge regular orders from McDonald's, were forced to raise their standards and because of that regular income stream they could afford to implement the changes necessary. In short they now had the cash to expand. This had an amazingly

Expand Your Brand

positive domino impact on the local economy and community as we were creating jobs. That's what I love about business: it really can be a creative and powerful web for positive change both locally and globally.

Remember your suppliers are part of your three-legged stool. Make your suppliers feel like they are part of your team. Get them involved with most of the pre-opening meetings. Invite them to launches, milestone celebrations and cultural or religious festivities. Invest time and energy in developing a good healthy business relationship with your suppliers.

Invest time and energy in developing a good healthy business relationship with your suppliers.

Key Points

- You are only as strong as your supply chain.

- Quality, reliability and competitive pricing are essential.

- Have a back-up plan in place.

- Get established safely – then use leverage to drive costs down and look at local supply chains.

- Logistics mapping relies on cost, location, reliable fast transport.

- Think profit whilst thinking about helping to support the local economy.

- Include your supply chain in your business community – both planning and celebrating.

CHAPTER
10

SUPPLY CHAIN PLUS

One of the biggest challenges you will experience as a world brand or large national brand is maintaining consistency and quality. I had to operate in many countries where regulations and protocols around food and hygiene were simply not yet established.

When I enquired in Fiji about the animal welfare laws my joint venture partner laughed. Although he was an animal lover he pointed out that Fiji was currently trying to implement human welfare laws, let alone take care of the chickens! Working around these issues was both challenging and rewarding. It brought new awareness to issues that were commonplace to the affluent West. We were often in countries where having some food on the table was the issue – food safety production never crossed their minds.

Tahiti had a large import tax to protect the local businesses, so we were forced to look for local produce suppliers. The supply chain team and the joint venture partner had to work extremely delicately and diplomatically to enforce higher standards. It was a great learning curve for both parties. Obviously we could not compromise on quality and yet needed to educate in a way that was non-judgmental and non-patronising. My core cross-cultural competencies came in very handy!

McDonald's Noumea New Caledonia.

First store in Fiji in Nadi.

In New Caledonia we were in some ways backed into a corner. We were unable to import any bread as the government has banned this. As we know, France and her sister territories have the finest bakers in the world. It was a question of patriotic pride (I am of course being very diplomatic here). We sourced a large bakery capable of our demand but we wanted to make a few small changes to align with the McDonald's quality and hygiene standards etc. This particular baker was supplying all the major branded shopping centres and grocery stores and quite frankly did not need to kowtow to our demands. Let's just say that our requests for better storage of the bun pans and some minor changes to the physical plant were met with a few expletives that we were not expecting. My French is very poor but I got the gist quite emphatically.

> Remember that often a closing door is simply asking you to turn around and look for another opening.

There is always a way and we managed to find it. Remember that often a closing door is simply asking you to turn around and look for another opening. But all of these issues are pressing and urgent and can, and do influence projected opening dates. That's why I always did strong reconnaissance. I had to know the lay of the land and the possible hurdles. I have cleared a few in my time, skimmed over the top of some and I'm not ashamed to say, knocked a couple over.

We had the same French pride around bread when we opened in Tahiti. We took a different angle when trying to find a bakery. We approached the local baker and offered to purchase new equipment and help set-up the production system. We enabled this baker to supply to us, and many others, at a greater speed and with improved cost efficiency.

We cut a deal to deduct the initial capital we had 'loaned' from the purchase price of the bread. It was a win-win that made everyone happy and made me exceptionally relieved.

Here I must give credit to the local joint venture partners. Negotiating as a big brand player can be exceptionally intimidating to many smaller countries or regions. Yet having a local joint venture partner as an intermediary is wise and sometimes essential.

I still smile sometimes when I think about government officials in customs departments. Once we were encouraged by an official not to import the fillet and chicken patties because he could get us a great deal with his brother-in-law. This provincial way of doing business has its charm and sometimes its nepotistic uses but giving away the control of quality and safety is not something you can afford to do. Your brand integrity is your business.

Big brand alliance can be tremendously powerful for both parties. It's a symbiotic relationship worth seeking out and nurturing. One of the biggest suppliers to McDonald's is Coca Cola. It's a very old marriage in many parts of the world. In the Pacific, because of excellent relationships with Coca Cola, we were able to cross-leverage our brands which saved a lot on advertising and marketing.

We were lucky in the sense that we had an exceptionally competent and dedicated supply chain team and quality assurance team. They were worth their weight in gold not just for the suppliers they sourced but also for the strong contingency plans that they had put in place. Contingency plans could range from freezer storage to stand-by suppliers. All avenues were taken care of, so that if one part of the chain broke we would not have to close for business.

Your foolproof supply chain ensures you stay open for business and the cash register is singing – in French, English or Tahitian. It does not matter what language it is, as long as the tune is Money!

Key Points

* Establish clear and healthy relationships with your local suppliers early in the set up of your brand – ask the locals.

* Avoid tactless and unprofessional rejection of local suppliers – you might need their assistance one day.

* Once you have the supplier that you are comfortable with, start to work with them and get them all the 'experts' to assist to get their production up to your standards.

* Sometimes the smaller guys are keener to have your business than the big guys. They may be more accommodating.

* Never assume small countries or small businesses are naïve or inexperienced. You might be able to share skills and knowledge.

* Be flexible with time and migration plans when you are negotiating with new-suppliers.

* Do not overwhelm potential suppliers with a 200-page document of your specifications. See what they do right, check it off your list and only present what needs adapting.

CHAPTER
11

RECRUITMENT AND TRAINING

McDonald's is a total people industry. Some services and products have little to do with people. It pays to examine what percentage of your business depends on the quality and attitude of your staff.

When you know how much of your business involves people contact; answering the phone, face-to-face time with the customer, management hierarchy, returns and complaints and so on, you will then know how much time you need to invest in accurate

Business is a lonely place when you only think of yourself – you are part of a dynamic web no matter how solo you think you fly!

and detailed recruitment and training. Of course some jobs can be learned in seconds and some take weeks or months. Obviously you invest more in recruitment and training for the positions that are the most difficult to replace.

When you go into a new country or a new territory, it sometimes pays to bring across some existing trained employees. I always wanted a fast and efficient team when I first opened the doors. It might cost a little more to bring in pre-trained employees but they were so invaluable at leading by example and training the new staff that it was worth it both in terms of time and money. For me, the brand impact is the most important factor: you only get one chance to make a first impression!

> For me, the brand impact is the most important factor: you only get one chance to make a first impression!

If going into a new culture you must learn all you can about the cultural norms. Be as detailed as possible. Learn things such as what is considered appropriate attire, including street, business or interview dress code. What are common greetings, formal and informal greetings, social etiquette and manners. We might have missed some great employees if we had applied the social norms of the US to the Pacific. What is considered lazy and not having made the effort in the US, is deemed casual, appropriate and confident in the Pacific.

Understand the local and national laws for your business. Find out about laws for hiring locals, how many hours they can work and what role unions will play in your business.

Both New Caledonia and Tahiti have strong unions and we had to have plans in place all the time to negotiate with them. I would advise setting up a meeting with unions before you even start recruiting. You need them on your side and they can be extremely informative and save you a lot of time and money in the long run.

McDonald's is unique as it is a systemised franchise business that operates in vastly different cultures and vastly different languages. Think about the complex web of recruitment, salaries, terms and conditions of contracts, worker's rights, unions (or lack of them), holiday times and pay that varies from one country to the next. And yet the McDonald's brand is uniformed in a familiar way with only slight cultural variations. The umbrella values and ethics keep the image of the global independent franchises consistent; and yet they are all individual. This conversely gives some freedom and creative licence for each country.

I have learned that work ethics and values vary greatly from country to country. It is imperative that you study your recruitment pool. Speak with agents and HR people and get good advice. Learn all there is to know about what makes this particular workforce motivated. Of course the common denominator is money. I always tried to pay the local workforce between 10 and 15 per cent above the national average to attract the best and the brightest and to secure longevity and promote loyalty.

Often in smaller countries training is grassroots and quite primitive. More often than not it meant that we were opening the first McDonald's restaurant in the country. So there was no other restaurant to train staff in and then bring them over. We would have to improvise. For example, in Fiji the staff were trained with cardboard-cut-out shapes of lettuce and cheese etc. They learned to speed dress burgers this way so as to avoid waste. For the Drive-Thru restaurants the managers would drive around and around the Drive-Thru placing complex orders until service and speed were perfected.

When we did finally open the Drive-Thru we realised that we also had to train the customers. People would drive up, order their food and then drive past the pick-up booth and drive off without their food. So we drew a map and instructions on how to use the Drive-Thru and did a mail out and even put it in the local paper. What might seem very obvious to one culture might be completely unknown to the next.

Because of the nature of the job and the hours, not everyone has the foresight to realise that working hard at the bottom might get you to somewhere impressive at the top. It's a common global phenomenon that we are producing the quick-fix generation.

Pre opening staff for Tahiti opening.

Keeping staff motivated and keeping staff retention high is always a challenge. I was against locking staff into contracts and believe there are far better ways to keep your team motivated and stimulated. Here are some of them:

- Build mutual trust and respect. Without your team you are nothing and without you your team are often floundering aimlessly.

- Build understanding. Getting your team to see things from different perspectives helps build mature working relationships. Teaching them to see difference as interesting rather than wrong often removes volatile right or wrong scenarios.

- Be interested in all your staff and learn their names, no matter how many!

- If you have an established brand ensure that your staff knows that they have been selected because you believe they can make a valuable contribution. Never give the attitude that they should be lucky to work for you because of your brand power or prestige.

- Build motivation and foresight. Your team needs to feel that their efforts are seen and rewarded and most importantly that there is a purpose. Set goals or rewards that mean something to them. Find out what motivates them individually. Abstract rhetoric and unrealistic goals will alienate members of your team and actually de-motivate them.

- Take time to train: make it matter. For example, I used to run a class for staff who were 15 to 16 year old and showed them the path they could take to get to be managing directors in the company or transfer those skills to another company. They might not aspire to be the MD of McDonald's but they might aspire to be the MD of a cool skateboard fashion range. I used to use real life examples of people like Charlie Bell who started out as a 15-year-old crew person and then went on to be the global CEO of McDonald's or Guy Russo who also started as a crew member and then went on to run McDonald's Australia and China.

- Focus on harnessing natural talents and leaning new skill-sets. We all want to be seen for who we are and the gifts we bring. We also need to keep on learning for our self-value to continue to grow. Either provide or initiate training programmes that will appeal to your team, especially your younger employees.

- Support your staff in their personal and professional development, especially when they get discouraged with personal, political or global events and impacts.

- Young employees have little relationship to the future. Help bridge the gap between impulse and instant gratification to wise and delayed gratification without sounding like a nagging parent. Teach them the concept of the bigger picture.

- Build your training around recognition and reward. Sometimes in smaller, poorer countries where cash-flow was critical we would ensure that rewards were never slashed. You can get creative with low cost rewards. However, make it something relevant and appropriate to the age and experience of your team.

- Have informal regular check-in sessions. Perhaps a buddy system will achieve this at very low cost.

- Ask your employees for feedback – what works and what doesn't and then publicly acknowledge them for any changes that are implemented, based on their suggestions.

- Make the work environment fun and diverse – implement a 12-month social plan as well as business and marketing plans.

- Where possible have a day each couple of months when leaders, senior management and management work on the floor with the crew or side-by-side with factory workers or junior office executives.

- Look at a benefits scheme – what perks can you offer your staff? It could be a gym membership discount. In Tahiti we had a motivational gym instructor train the staff once a week.

- We gave many of the staff the opportunity to train overseas. This was a huge bonus and motivational incentive. Many of the employees had never left their hometown.

- When looking at time off respect other cultures traditions around births, deaths, weddings and other key events.

Support your staff in their personal and professional development, especially when they get discouraged with personal, political or global events and impacts.

Key Points

- Establish how much of a people business you are.

- If you skimp on training at the start you will pay in the end.

- Consider recruiting pre-trained staff for the initial start-up phase.

- Study a country's cultural norms, work values and ethics.

- Make friends with the unions before recruitment starts.

- You don't need elaborate or sophisticated training tools – get creative and keep it simple.

- Your team is made up of individuals. Treat them that way!

- Consider training the customer – make your brand and your systems super user-friendly.

> Your team is made up of individuals. Treat them that way!

- Training is something you do with people, not to people.

- Training is not a one-way relationship; it is a relationship in which both parties share responsibility.

- Training is not a one off process but an ongoing process.

- Continuous learning should be woven into the everyday fabric of your business if you want to achieve long lasting results.

CHAPTER
12

MANAGEMENT DEVELOPMENT AND GROOMING

The ability to discover potential new managers and to groom them for future expansion projects is one of the smartest things you can do in business. When you move your brand into a new territory or country you will need a proficient and cohesive management team.

Ensuring that the management team is bursting with initiative, competency and ambition will guarantee dynamic progress. You will be paying them more to do more and certainly have more responsibility. Because you have invested time and money in their training, you will obviously want to keep them.

New staff, management or crew have their own start-up costs. It is essential that you allocate money for their in-depth and personalised training. The more you can minimize staff and management turnover, the more profits you can retain. I would suggest hiring some locals as trainee management as well as bringing in some experienced managers from established overseas or interstate markets. When building your team for a new country, choose people who are curious, adaptable, from mixed backgrounds and respectful of other cultures and customs.

If you do bring in overseas management you will really need to take care of them. Expats have the adventure and opportunity for something new, but they are often in some sort of culture shock themselves and want to go home after a few months. They need particular care and attention. Firstly it has to be financially worth it for them and secondly they will need to feel part of a community right away. There are usually strong expat networks. Make time and effort to plug into these to ease your new managers into their foreign surroundings.

Bringing in an expat work force can be very expensive. It's wise to have a one to two year contract and a realistic migration plan to eventually have only local people employed. If you are looking at joint venture or franchise partners this will please them. They of course have a great interest in supporting the local economy.

Your talent is your business. We often referred to the potential management people as the 'talent'. Make no mistake about it, in both a product and service industry; your talent is your business. Getting the magic right here can make all the difference with both profits and a great working environment. Having a recognisable brand often makes the jobs more attractive. A big brand offers job security and a career path as well as prestige.

In Fiji we had over 5,000 applications to work as crew. There was no shortage of staff, but I spent time looking for the right combinations and the most promising. Within your particular field you will learn what type of personality and level of experience and education will best suit each position. Your specific goal is to get the right talent who will stay in their job for as long as possible.

It is important to get to know the talent in your organisation. List the key people in your organisation and sort them into two categories: leaders and followers. Then break them down into subsets. You will need a combination of all six subsets listed below to make up the magic mix. You don't want too many chiefs and not enough Indians or vice versa!

- Leaders with initiative

- Followers with initiative

- Leaders with initiative and ambition

- Followers with initiative and ambition

- Leaders with initiative, ambition and an aptitude to learn and instruct.

- Followers with initiative, ambition and an aptitude to learn and instruct.

Opening team of Managers.

If you do not have the skills to recruit a combination of personality types for your specific roles, then contact a recruitment agency. The clearer you are about what you need and why, the more certain you are of getting what you want. When you have identified your leaders and followers with initiative, ambition and an aptitude to learn and instruct, then dedicate more time and training to them. It's not playing favourites, it's just playing smart and reflecting back the energy and enthusiasm that they are putting in.

Monitor the team; identify key-people, what makes them tick and what are their specific needs and goals. At an early stage identify who merits management investment, grooming and development. Set up in-house fast track programmes, as this can be a more tangible way to monitor staff's progress. If it takes the average full-time employee 12 months to be proficient in all areas of a particular programme, then challenge your key people to do it in less time. Set key-milestones on the programme and ensure follow up. Sometimes the programme may need to be accelerated or slowed down. You will need to be flexible, fair, and diplomatic and support equal opportunity.

Recruitment forecasting is always necessary when expanding your brand. Get a clear sense of how many staff you need, how many can you afford and whether there are enough people to cover illness and sick-day phone-ins. Map out a talent plan – write down ideal scenarios and aim to actualise them. I had great intuition in staff selection and especially management selection; after all I was once young and on the bottom rung.

An essential strategy in management development is to make your leaders accountable. Their rewards should be based on how well they have performed within the talent development programme. As with most performance-based and initiative-based programmes, you are often looking for things that are not on the list. Doing your job well is what is expected of you. Going above and beyond the call of duty is worthy of recognition and reward.

Participate in professional organisations where you will meet new young talent. Develop and maintain strong relationships with recruiters and universities. University graduation fairs are a good opportunity to present your career paths and enlist. We would often have open days to allow potential management to see the business in action and present career paths.

In the case of McDonald's, flipping burgers and supersizing orders is not the incentive. Rather it is the fast-track career opportunities and the training.

The performance pressure for new employees is often greater with a prestigious brand or an overseas brand. They will always remember their first day on the job, so make sure you allocate time to help them with their orientation. In some cases, with the opening in a new country, you might have to do a huge orientation of between 100 to 150 people. Even with large numbers it is imperative to be exceptionally well organised with training plans, orientation handouts, health and safety, job description and expectations.

Give every single new employee the impression that they are regarded as an individual. This makes all the difference. Name tags, actually using their name and eye contact goes a long, long way!

Buddy systems work exceptionally well when they are cross roles. By that I mean, have a team leader buddy a crewmember. I always enforced that every single job was as important as the next in the greater workings of the business. Equality is a state of mind and not defined by the type of work you do.

Key Points

- Keep an eye out for management talent and potential.

- Ensure you have a finely tuned respectful and fair management team.

- Employ already trained management with a clear migration plan and time frame to employ local management.

- Get people with the right talent to stay in their role or with the company for as long as possible.

- Look at leaders and followers and what other qualities they bring.

- Consider recruitment agencies if you need help in creating your dream team.

- Sell your career path, training and opportunity, not specific job titles.

- Treat every employee as an individual, especially when they work in large teams where they can be easily invisible.

- Create internal informal support for employees, buddy systems with management and leaders and regular check-in sessions as well as formal appraisal sessions.

- Equality is everything.

CHAPTER

13

JOINT VENTURE PARTNERS, LICENSEES AND FRANCHISE SYSTEMS

Partnering can have its pros and cons, but it's a great idea when going into a new country or territory. Having a local partner with the same amount of investment as you takes an enormous amount of pressure off. It's like going into the heart of Amazonian unchartered territory with your own guide and protector.

Dealing with partnerships is a huge topic and there are many good books about the varying subjects, legal splits and contracts. There are various ways to partner in business including a 50 per cent split in investment and start-up costs and subsequently a 50 per cent share in profits – often called a joint venture (JV). Among other alternatives is the development license (DL), whereby the partner finances the whole project and pays a percentage from sales to the parent company.

McDonald's set a trend and now there are many variations on the franchise theme. Research which model will work best for you both right now and also in the future expanded business setup.

The franchise enterprise pioneered by McDonald's has been replicated throughout the world. It's a complicated system that varies from country to country – especially legally. If you do want to go down this track you will need to be very well informed and have experienced lawyers who work specifically with joint venture in that particular country or territory.

The main, essential starting point is the watertight legal contract. Fortunately as the world is more and more used to this kind of business partnering, it is becoming easier to obtain standardised contracts quickly and inexpensively. But it's a step that you cannot miss – no matter how much you trust your new partner or how much money you might save.

Be flexible – sometimes you may find the 'perfect' partner who may not be able to have the same initial financial investment. Either re-adjust the percentage ratio or have a plan in place whereby the partner can buy the rest of the shares back in the future.

Stay open and look for particular qualities that perhaps the individual country needs or perhaps qualities that can compliment your own. There are often customs and ways of doing business that you might never understand no matter how hard you try or how long you live in the new culture.

I always followed my gut feeling as well as doing extensive background research when searching for, and selecting the right JV partner for a new territory. When you are narrowing down who you might work with as a partner it's a good idea to spend time in their existing companies. Being inside their operations can give a more accurate reading of how they actually implement systems, procedures and most importantly how they manage people.

I once spent some time at the offices of a very promising partner until I began to notice little memos posted all over the workplace, things like, 'Do this or you're fired' or 'Forget this and it comes out of your wages'. Needless to say, I realised we were not compatible with regards to people management.

Olivier Loyant Partner in Tahiti.

Here are a few examples of what I looked for in a JV partner. Each country's needs were specific but on the whole these were the most important prerequisites:

- An already established successful business reputation in the community.

- Well connected and respected in the business community.

- Experience working with big brands and big corporations.

- Attributes and or assets that they can bring to the table with regards to already established relationships with bigger brands and the wider business community.

- Extensive training or the ability to learn quickly with flexibility and drive.

- An approved, prime, workable store location.

- A council-approved infrastructure for building and parking.

- A clear or neutral standing in local and national politics.

- A strong existing customer base.

- A clear and healthy present and track record with the unions.

- A commitment to work the business with a set number of hours.

- A long-term commitment, a positive attitude and solution focused.

- A commitment to ongoing training and refresher courses.

- A well tuned business intuition and current business know-how.

- A healthy mind, body and spirit.

- A recognition that what they lack in things like experience and age will need to be balanced with dedication and enthusiasm.

- A realistic assessment of their age, stamina and what is required for a start-up commitment.

- A feeling of wider support both personally and professionally.

- Capital with enough cash flow to support the business for one to two years.

- Mutual compatibility to sustain a close and long working relationship.

- The ability to listen, reflect and be non-reactive.

> A succession plan – someone they can leave the business to who knows and is involved in the business.

- A display of mutual values, loyalty and commitment.

- A strong leader with instruction and by example.

- A succession plan – someone they can leave the business to who knows and is involved in the business.

Hans Joe Keil, partner for Samoa.

CHAPTER
14

MANAGE, MONITOR AND MENTOR

I often think that people are confused about KPIs. Firstly the acronym means Key Performance Indicators. It's a brilliant method used to monitor business achievements or goals and staff achievements.

> When you expand you have to let others learn to take the helm. Ensure that those new captains sail as well as, if not better, than you do!

I want to focus here on staff progress and management. KPIs are an effective tool to manage staff and help them towards managing themselves. When a staff member takes full responsibility for their role, even takes pride in it, then you are looking at management material, possible executive leadership qualities. But most importantly you are looking at a well-run business that needs little supervision. You then get to spend more time on growing the business rather than more time on the business basics and ongoing maintenance.

Remember that KPI's need to be SMARRT:

- specific

- measurable

Expand Your Brand

- achievable

- result-orientated

- relevant

- time based

During staff appraisals the KPI map is used to benchmark progress and failings. It gives a much fairer analysis of how things actually are. The staff gets a voice and a much more direct understanding of what is asked of them and what they can achieve. It's a measuring tool designed to help the staff member identify core strengths and skill gaps.

Predominantly, there are three main areas managers need to look at with regards to their staff:

- Where they might need support and further training.

- Where they are possibly overqualified and might be better used elsewhere within the company structure.

- Where it might be better for all concerned for the staff member to look for another job.

Knowing exactly how much time to fairly and legally invest in staff is a great art. This skill and discernment often comes from direct experience, and a lot of it. I believe that because I worked my way up with McDonald's, I witnessed every cross-section of personality types, from the ambitious conscientious 'yes' people like me, to the apathetic 'get me out of here' types. I literally worked with every type of human being. It was a learned and honed skill that would serve me very well in my long years of management.

Of course some industries have a higher turnover of staff than others, but it all costs money. The lower the staff turnover, the higher the profits. It's that simple.

Lisa Ransom.

Poor staff management can be an enormous drain on resources, time and money. It's vital that when contracts are written the new staff member or the promoted staff member acknowledges and agrees to what is asked of them. This has been a strategy that has really worked for me. I have always encouraged and been supportive of my team's personal and professional growth but never at the cost of the business.

It might sound a little harsh at first but when you think about it, it's a win-win for both parties. As the old saying goes: sometimes there's no use flogging a dead horse. The flogger gets exhausted and the horse gets deader!

I have a great track record with my staff. I do believe in taking care of them. I believe it's essential. And yet I am a little old fashioned in the sense that I believe that respect should be earned and not automatically given. It's a two-way street. They need to earn my respect and simultaneously I need to earn theirs. Then within that framework – KPIs can be written and implemented.

Key Points

- Work out your KPIs both financial and non-financial.

- Get specific – although they may change slightly you usually only have to do this once for each job description.

- Make KPIs known to your team. These indicators should never come as a surprise to employees, for example at a performance review.

- Get each staff member to acknowledge and agree to what is asked of them and to recognise when their appraisal with KPIs is due.

- KPIs need to be SMARRT.

- Be fair but be realistic.

- Earn your respect and encourage your team to do the same.

CHAPTER
15

CULTURAL COMPETENCE

One of the first ways to analyse your level of cultural competency is to be very honest with yourself and your own social conditioning. We all come with a cultural overlay imprinted upon us by social mores, religious overtones, peer pressure and now, more than ever, global influence.

Most of us have some covert hidden beliefs that perhaps might need an upgrade. For example we may believe the stereotypes that older workers will not adapt to change; accountants have no feelings or French people are arrogant. We may trot out clichés such as men are less sensitive than woman or men are better drivers.

It is subtle prejudice like these that undermine equality in life. They appear harmless when in fact they are not. To be a great leader of a brand in a global community you must question beliefs – your own beliefs and culturally-prescribed beliefs. Some we can take on, some we reject and some we have to accept. As a leader you need to push yourself to understand more about the cultural issues. This will help you appreciate, understand and maximize the talents of people who differ from you in culture, race, religion, gender and age.

Seek out and establish relationships with people who are different from you within the work place. Always consider your actions from the other's point of view. For example, in cultures where it is frowned upon to be seen as weak or needing help, people will never ask for assistance. It's often about losing face publicly. In this case you could ask for a private meeting and elicit where an employee may need help or support.

Here are some tips:

- Cultural competency needs to reach across to marketing and brand relevant placement. Bring the culture to the brand and not just the brand to the culture.

- The brand image and management must be in the hands of the culturally competent and the locals.

- Often cultural competency is having the courage to ask the right questions or admit a skill gap.

- Get the heads of departments in different countries to work together.

- Expand your definition of diversity beyond skin colour and national origin.

- Get diverse perspectives from friends, colleagues and advisers who are part of or know the hurdles of living in a particular culture.

- Always encourage and support people from diverse backgrounds to succeed within your company, even if they need a little extra time and support.

- Have an open door policy.

The rules apply equally to people at all levels. Always appoint a senior person above you as the one who can take care of complaints or issues about you. People need to feel safe to express their concerns or frustrations.

Opening day in Tahiti.

As well as managing cultural diplomacy with your core team and management team, you will also have to know how to liaise with your partners. When the money and the good times are rolling in there is often little tension, but when there are issues, people, out of fear, often display hidden cultural or character traits that may surprise you. You might have to terminate a contract and learn how to do that within the cultural constraints.

Being culturally sensitive in all your business transactions will ultimately allow you to conduct what might be sticky business with a clean conscience. No matter what the issues are, always highlight that you are looking for a 'cure'. Give fair opportunities for your team and partners to change. Always leave a paper trail and have all delicate conversations witnessed. Never challenge employees or your JV partners in front of colleagues.

At the time of writing this there are over 32,000 McDonald's restaurants in more than 117 countries. Can you imagine the cultural diversity? I learned that the basic human needs of being appreciated, encouraged, supported and seen for what you do well is the only way to glue a team together in productivity and job-satisfaction.

Key points

- Be sensitive and aware of inequality and social prejudice. Through example illustrate the way of equality and fairness.

- Look for the merits of every person before you focus on their skill-gaps.

- Cultivate a work culture of acceptance, respect and appreciation of difference.

- Set up penalty and warnings for people who act disrespectfully and inappropriately. Have a zero tolerance level for discrimination of any kind.

- Encourage diversity and working together across cultures.

I learned that the basic human needs of being appreciated, encouraged, supported and seen for what you do well is the only way to glue a team together in productivity and job-satisfaction.

CHAPTER
16

LOST IN TRANSLATION: COMMUNICATIONS

"Think like a wise man but communicate in the language of the people." - William Butler Yeats

It might sound really obvious, but many people simply do not think about what language they would like to conduct business in. Of course the day-to-day store business is conducted in the local language and trades in the local currency. But often business meetings and management training is carried out in another language. In McDonald's case, it's English.

Straight away you have identified that you will need a bilingual assistant. Trust me it really helps. In the early days always check every translation even for the smallest memo; sometimes what we say is not what we mean.

By way of illustration, when an order is taken with a slight irregularity, say for example, a Big Mac with no cheese, we call this a 'grill order'. On the opening day in Samoa it was hot and really busy. I was running around lubricating the wheels of industry and closing gaps when I noticed one customer who was waiting a long time and it transpired that he was waiting for a 'grill order'. I started shouting, 'Come on, get the grill out. I want the grill out now!' or words to that effect.

Fiji Laucala Bay restaurant.

After some time, I noticed that everything was slowing down. Like really slow. So I went into the kitchen and found four chefs trying to get the grill out. No, I mean the big apparatus for cooking the food. There were four strong Samoan guys about to pull the grill up from the floor and out of the wall. I screamed, 'Stop! What are you doing?' They looked at me in disbelief, 'We are getting the grill out just like you asked!'

Never assume that just because you are an established brand, everyone will be familiar with the way you present or operate your business. It's essential to conduct surveys and do research to find out what they know or what they assume about your brand.

Humans are very good at adding two and two and getting seven.

> **Never assume that just because you are an established brand, everyone will be familiar with the way you present or operate your business.**

We made a grave assumption in Fiji: somehow we missed the fact that half the Fijian population were Fijian Indians and a large percentage of them, due to religious reasons, do not eat beef. On the first day we were met with countless complaints about the cheeseburger. I tasted a few and they were great. As the manager slowed down and I became present enough to hear what he was actually saying, I could not believe my ears. The complaint was about false advertising and misrepresentation.

American Samoa 10th year anniversary, second from left Charlie Tautolo partner.

When they ordered a cheeseburger they did not expect it to come with beef but only cheese. It was obvious to us, and equally obvious to them, what ingredients a cheeseburger contained – right? We had to act extremely quickly and have all the menu boards and signage updated to say, 'Contains beef'.

I remember on the morning of the opening of the first restaurant in Fiji we had all been working like crazy to get ready. With about one hour to go before the opening an employee came up to me and asked me what I wanted him to

Expand Your Brand

do for the day as he was on the staff roster, but without a job description. I did not have the time to sort it out there and then so I improvised. I looked around and spotted a garbage bin on wheels that McDonald's use for their car park and immediate surrounds. I asked him to make sure that he got all the litter from around the area.

The day was chaotic but it went relatively well. Later on that evening around 5pm, when I was heading back to my hotel for a fresh change of clothes, I saw the same employee picking up the garbage some six kilometres away from the restaurant. I could not believe my eyes. I asked him what he was doing and he said, 'Cleaning up the area boss!' I commended him on his initiative and dedication, gave him the money for a taxi home and told him we'd deal with the bin in the morning.

Key Points

* Be clear, be specific, be simple.

* Ensure that you have a bilingual partner or assistant in foreign countries.

* Ask for some instructions to be repeated back to you.

* Assume your team are hearing something for the first time until you find a clear communication channel and a frequency that everyone understands.

* Always recap your meetings and conversations in 24 to 48 hours of the event happening. Write things on memos in large print for the staff locker rooms.

* Learn some local common phrases and have fun with communication.

CHAPTER
17

BURKA² AND LARGE FRIES PLEASE!

"Two roads diverged in a wood and I took the one less travelled, and that has made all the difference." - Robert Frost

I am not sure where to begin with the Arabian McDonald's epic that was Saudi Arabia. I had just begun to call Australia home and had really gotten used to the bizarre accent and strange idiosyncrasies of the Australian way of life when the opportunity to work in Saudi came along. It was such a chaotic and unpredictable venture that when I begin to tell of my time there I'm quite sure nobody will believe me. It's so often implausible but it really, truly happened! Despite the challenges, it's the one country that makes me smile the most. Hindsight is a safe place indeed to have a good laugh.

In many ways it was the most challenging in terms of working within a cultural structure that was so completely alien to me. Even the glorious chaos of India cannot prepare you for the rules and social mores of a country like Saudi Arabia. My passion to expand into new countries was both ignited and tested here.

The market research and surveys had indicated that Saudi was ripe for McDonald's. We soon learned that that was an understatement. We had the perfect business. Can you imagine having security guards at the doors of the store to limit the number of people that entered the restaurant during busy periods? Outside we had to deploy a maze-like queuing system, normally reserved for airport check-in or tight security processes. We were immediately organising our progressive and speedy expansion plan.

As there are no nightclubs in Saudi Arabia and there is a very strict policing of socialising and courting between men and women, McDonald's was seen by the religious police as a possible venue for irreligious activities. Therefore we were policed from opening time to closing time. Everything was so new and unfamiliar that our negotiating strategies had to be realigned and adapted. We absolutely respected the Saudi culture and we were doing our best to get it right, but it wasn't always that simple. I remember thinking just that whilst sitting in a Saudi jail whilst reassuring the rest of my staff, who had also been arrested, that we would all be just fine!

Being in jail or jail-breaking my staff was not part of my training at McDonald's. There was of course no protocol to follow except to think on my feet. The crimes we were accused of, on a fairly regular basis, were breaking cultural and religious law. It might have been something as innocent as a male member of staff forgetting and speaking directly to a female customer. If this was witnessed by the religious police the whole crew would be arrested and before you could say, 'I'll have fries with that!', we were all being loaded into vans. This often happened in peak trading hours.

I quickly developed a system to handle these situations by calling my relief manager and he would rally those crew who were not in jail and arrange for them to be at the restaurant within minutes. An average McDonald's store would operate with five to eight managers and approximately 40 to 60 crew members. Saudi had 45 managers and more than 200 crew, so you can imagine the huge logistics involved in changing over the entire team before the next customer could place their order! Meanwhile, back at the police station, I would have to sign a declaration stating that we were deeply sorry that we had broken Islamic Law and we were subsequently set free.

We had to build two separate dining areas; one for the men and one for the women and families. In the women's and family areas we also had to build family booths that were completely private, so that the women could eat without being seen. Women were not allowed to speak with any men unless they were related or they were officially engaged. I am known for my open and friendly nature. It was very difficult to 'ignore' one half of my clientele. But again my choice was to comply or go straight to jail!

We had to employ staff from other countries and other religious backgrounds. For example Saudi women are not allowed to work in Saudi Arabia but they cannot be served by a man either. So we were forced to employ outside of the local sphere. It was quite an operation recruiting and training staff in the Philippines and then flying them out on two-year contracts. Management were picked from already established countries, mostly the United States or Europe. It was a mash of cultures, ideal or not ideal, this is how it was. We did our best and hoped for the best.

In the beginning the local Saudi kids would come in and stare at the menu, they would then send their drivers in to buy the food. They would usually get one of everything on the menu.

Sometimes another kid would compete with his friend and order two of everything off the menu. It was easy enough until it came to the drinks; they wanted one or two in each size, same with the fries, small, medium and large. The cash register sang and the kids were happy.

I remember everything was running as smoothly as it possibly could when we were suddenly raided because of the Nugget Sauce. At first I was bemused when we were told that the wine flavouring, although the sauce contained no alcohol, was against Islamic Law. We had to be witnessed in throwing them all in the garbage.

I would often be in jail dressed in my suit and tie seated next to bleeding and dishevelled men. I would imagine what they were thinking: that I must have committed some heinous crime. I was almost too embarrassed to tell them I was in for selling Big Macs with French fries.

Our operating agreement required us to close five times a day for prayers. At least the crew had good breaks or we could catch up on essential ordering, or cleaning. We made it work for us too. It is sometimes difficult to not judge but simply accept. This is a great lesson that I learned in Saudi. I also learnt that no matter how much I loved McDonald's, I wouldn't kill for a French fry!

Key Points

- Understand the local cultural and religious mores before you launch your brand. Stay neutral and remember you are there for business.

- Have a great back-up plan that works within your budget.

- Ensure your suppliers have all their products certified and approved by the local customs and law.

- Align with a culture-smart joint venture partner, who has an understanding of your brand or business and a firm belief in the compatibility of it with the new terrain.

- Remain respectful of difference no matter how great.

- Never admit your Big Mac crime to a mass murderer whilst sharing a locked cell.

Understand the local cultural and religious mores before you launch your brand. Stay neutral and remember you are there for business.

---

[2] Burka: an all-enveloping cloak that covers the body and head that is worn by some Muslim women. The garment has small slits for the eyes.

CHAPTER
18

SHOE-STRING MARKETING

If my career hadn't gone the way of operations and management, I seriously would have liked to work in marketing. I love creative people and the energy and the tireless ability to refresh a brand and give it a makeover.

McDonald's has been reinventing itself for over 60 years. I admire the way global marketing morphs and merges with individual countries by learning their customs, their language and their sense of humour.

In smaller countries we had a very limited marketing and advertising budget. Most brands would recommend a marketing budget of three to seven per cent of sales, so when you are launching you are very limited. It all comes out of your start-up fund. Really have a look at the most effective way to manage your start-up advertising and marketing campaign.

A brand like McDonald's of course has a head start: alongside Coca Cola it's one of the most recognisable brands in the world. Yet still, it needs to compete and win over customers. New customers still need to know where you are and your hours of opening. Letter drops or a page in the local paper are cheap and effective. And these days there are all sorts of creative ways to market with YouTube, Twitter, Facebook and LinkedIn.

Creative Marketing-McDonald's Fiji Freezer truck.

The Hero at work.

Expand Your Brand

You don't have to spend a fortune – just get creative. Getting your team involved is a great idea for some creative participation. Who knows what they might come up with? Then when sales increase, so too does the marketing and advertising budget.

I always liked the local advertising to reflect something about the local culture or specific cultural events. McDonald's would sponsor Samoa for the Pacific Island Beauty Pageant, which is one of the biggest events in the country. The winner became the brand ambassador for the next year as well as continuing with her other responsibilities. She had celebrity status for 12 months and her face on billboards and often alongside the golden arches.

The budget allocated to developing a 30-second commercial in Australia could be the annual marketing budget for a country like Samoa. I remember in Samoa we tracked down an editing studio in a nearby university. At the time it was the only editing studio in the entire country! I would hire some local celebrities or models and pay them with Big Mac Vouchers; enough to feed their families for a whole week. We would then use the US McDonald's Film and TV advertisements and splice them with the local actors, celebrities and models. It worked exceptionally well and the local people really responded. They felt included, represented and part of it. It would Mac their day!

Marketing in the first year needs to create and then build upon brand awareness. I would always keep menus really simple when we opened. Too much choice at the front counter was confusing and slowed operations right down. Because the profit margins are usually lower, fast food restaurants can only stay afloat by having high turnover of customers, therefore maximising service time is critical.

New Caledonia - Koutio Store.

President of Tahiti Gaston Flosse (center) to open the first McDonald's in the country.

Expand Your Brand

Using pictures of the products with corresponding numbers facilitated fluid communication and avoided language barrier issues. As the years went by, more and more choices were added. Some stores waited between five and ten years before adding the breakfast menu.

I have learned a lot about marketing from our joint venture partners. Our Fijian partner Craig had commented on how few bins there were in the park. He struck a deal with council and had more bins put in the park all with the McDonald's logo. It's simple things like that that are so cost effective and really make a difference. Craig was also very good at negotiating with people to have directional billboards erected close to the restaurants. As McDonald's was such a novelty at the time, his bartering would often include some very popular Big Mac vouchers redeemable in store.

Olivier, our Tahitian partner, cleverly leveraged some very simple promotional tools. First of all, he designed artwork for his tray-mats (which is a paper liner for the portable trays used to carry food from the counter to your table). The tray-mat featured all of his core products that were available at the counter. He then took the same artwork and had it resized for a letterbox drop to local households and, just for good measure, he arranged for the same design to appear in the local newspaper. One payment for graphic design, one bulk printing bill, one uniform branding message and many uses: it worked like a charm.

In the Middle East I had the 'brilliant' idea to have the logo emblazoned in bold on all the company cars. I quickly had to remove them when we were getting reports that McDonald's cars were being seen speeding all over the city. Bad publicity in this case was not good publicity. Maybe we should have asked the drivers at interview about their aspirations towards the Formula One Challenge.

Patrick in Noumea would launch all his products using 25 to 30 billboards. The French people and the French territories respond well to billboards. Patrick figured this out early on, so started his own billboard company. Smart move!

There will be three basic marketing strategies when you take your brand into a new country or territory.

- Pre-Opening: Build Brand Awareness for up to six months before you open.

- Opening: Make a big splash with your marketing and advertising campaign.

- On-going maintenance campaigns: Market new products and special offers.

Once you have successfully launched your business I recommend getting into the habit of developing a Marketing Calendar for the following 12- month period. Your plan should include both global as well as local holidays, festivities and important cultural events. It is relatively easy to download calendars and templates from the internet by visiting national tourism sites.

In the first couple of years of operating in a new territory, try to keep your marketing messages simple and direct. Emphasising and re-emphasising who you are and what you are offering is the most cost-effective way to spend your marketing bucks. Look for a couple of strategic sponsorship deals that signal to the broader community that you are a part of their lives, and that your business cares about more than what you can sell them.

Key Points

- Be as creative as you can with your marketing plans. Look for ways to leverage what you have so that you can get more bang for your buck!

- Keep the start-up product line limited to core products.

- Develop a local network of talent and suppliers as quickly as you can. The time invested will pay big dividends.

- Television campaigns (TVC'S) are very expensive to produce. Find a way to use the basic template for a campaign that has worked successfully in a developed market, and customise it to feature local talent and products.

> Keep the start-up product line limited to core products.

- Carefully consider the most appropriate advertising method for different regions e.g. TV, local radio, newspapers, billboards or banners. Remember you want to make a big impact on your customers, but your budget might not match.

- Prepare a great marketing calendar for the following 12 months and make sure it has global and local relevance.

CHAPTER
19

COMPETITIVE BY NATURE

Many companies become their own worst enemy. They get complacent and take their eyes off the ball. They forget their core values, they forget about maintenance and they wonder why their reputation is sliding down alongside profits. Then in lazy bewilderment they scratch their head at the increased sales their competitors are enjoying and wonder what the hell happened.

While I believe that children should be taught that it's not all about winning; I believe that they should be encouraged to be their best at all times. And that naturally means sometimes being the best. At least the best at what you do. It does not mean that you are better than anyone else. It simply means that you are better at x, y or z. If something is measurable, then it's inevitably going to invite a few superlatives: fastest, smartest, wittiest, brainiest, the most philosophical, the most daring, the most ambitious, the most entrepreneurial and so on.

In my opinion there is nothing shameful about being competitive. It's the magic fuel of sport. Being competitive on the playing field is expected and therefore acceptable and normalised. As long as you can lose with a smile on your face and offer a genuine congratulatory handshake to your opponent, it's permissible to be overtly zealous about kicking your opponent's ass. You can be as expressive as you want about how you would like your nemesis to go down. It's part of getting in the zone. It's part of psyching each other out. Boxers are notorious for this.

Yet in business, unless we say 'healthy competition', people get suspicious of our ethics and our motives. I believe in ethical fair play all the way. But I do mean all the way. I have always wanted to win. I actually enjoy it. I enjoy motivating a team towards targets and goals. I enjoy the thrill of the bonus or the reward at the other end. In short, I love the challenge. I love how competition drives and shapes the product and therefore affects the market. In turn the market can have a dramatic impact on the shape of the product. It's a game of choices, chances and charmers. This is how progress manifests.

I reconcile my competitive desire to be the best by turning it on my business and myself. Strange logic maybe – but it works! It's like a weird sort of one-upmanship – except you firstly target your own business. Identify what you do very well. Then ask how can you surpass that. How can you compete with your own product or service? It keeps the creative flow and pre-empts a strike or counter attack by your opponents.

Secondly, I target the competition. I look at what they do well or what they do similarly to us or what do they do better. Then I look at ways to compete and ultimately beat them. Look at where you want to position yourself: aggressive forward or back-foot defence? If you only play defence and counter attack you will lose sight of initiative and the pioneering spirit. In some ways you lose belief in your vision and integrity. I leave the gloves on and fight fair. In that way both sides have the opportunity to raise the standard for each other thus taking both businesses to higher and more profitable ground.

KFC on Friday.

McDonald's the following Monday.

Expand Your Brand

It would be a very unsatisfying fight with only one contestant in the ring. Competitors are a wonderful mirror reflecting your particular business and also the market. And if competitors are one step ahead I look at it as though they are testing the market, often taking big risks. I sit back and see if that risk will pay off. And when it doesn't, I lose nothing. When it does I execute the counter attack – something better!

I also want to reiterate what I said about ethics. After all, a business is a hub of humans with families and loved ones. I never lose sight of this. Take for example KFC, a worthy opponent of McDonald's, who were the first fast-food restaurant to arrive in Tahiti. McDonald's came in six months later. I learned a lot from the KFC crew and had a lot of respect for them. But the town was not big enough for both of us. We spurred each other on and each did our best. In the end of course the customer is the ultimate umpire. This time my team and I won. Within two years KFC Tahiti had closed down.

In a friendly and even altruistic way we took over the KFC building, rebranded it into a McDonald's and opened up shop. I had made it a priority to give the KFC staff and management the opportunity to work for McDonald's. They were already trained and needed a job. It worked for all concerned.

> It's easy to 'win' – improve on quality, service, cleanliness and value!

Key Points

- Just because you are not the first brand of your type to enter a new territory it does not mean that you can't be first in sales and popularity.

- It's easy to 'win' – improve on quality, service, cleanliness and value!

- Make things swifter and more economical. Leave less room for error and more time for goal setting and rewards.

- Use your competitor to benchmark value and pricing if you have comparable products, for example the McChicken, Chicken McNuggets and KFC's Chicken Wings.

- Ask the customer! Don't be afraid to ask them directly for comparisons. Know your customer.

- We conducted focus groups and asked customers what they thought of McDonald's compared to KFC. Believe me, most people have no problem telling you what they really think and this takes all the guess work out of future menu or marketing decisions.

- Focus your team on the marketing plan, the strategy and the goals. We had a 12-month marketing plan with chicken. We went head-to-head with KFC to win customers over – and it worked.

- Include a regular audit of your competitors, like a 'secret shopper'. Your focus should be on your own goals, but you should always know what your competitors are up to!

- Try and keep everyone happy. There was no bad press about the closure of our rival or about McDonald's taking over in Tahiti. It was strictly business and we took over the lease of the building and re-employed staff. This level of diplomacy is paramount in a small country or territory.

CHAPTER
20

THE REAL DEAL

"The leader shows that style is no substitute for substance." - Lao Tzu

What other people think of you is none of your business – except when you are in business; then what other people think about you is absolutely your business.

It's a little bit of a mind-bending statement. But when you unpack it you will see the validity in it. It's loaded with good advice and philosophical mastery.

Firstly, it's a great message about **staying in integrity** with what you believe and what you are doing. You will always have people who will argue that you could be doing things in a better or different way. They will give their opinions freely and try to undermine your work, goals and vision.

Sometimes it's just the nature of human beings to criticise negatively and make futile comparisons, and this is often magnified when working for a large corporation. The message is clear here: do not get preoccupied with the negativity that some people might throw at you. Make that literally none of your business.

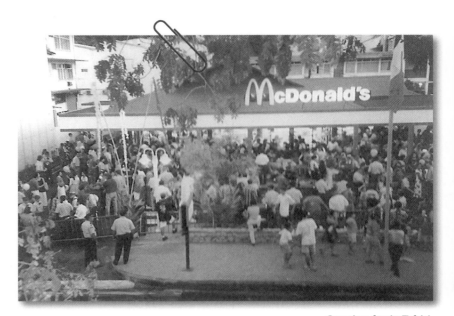

Opening day in Tahiti.

My last day in Tahiti.

Expand Your Brand

Secondly, the message is asking you to seek out and look for criticism that may be useful about your business. In my opinion, most executives are scared of customers and often erect an invisible wall to keep them at bay. The McDonald's culture openly encouraged all employees to engage with customers as frequently as possible. I genuinely believe this is one of the most beneficial things you can do.

Openly ask for feedback. Ask what could you do better and how and why? The more you listen to your customers the more chances you will have of seeing common threads. It's the most productive and cost-effective market research there is. Make your customers' opinions and feedback count. Listen, listen and then listen some more!

Thirdly, the statement alludes to the fact that, as a business owner or Joint Venture Partner, you are inextricably linked to your business. You are representing your business 24/7. You are directly and indirectly a broadcasting station about your brand and the way you operate. As a figurehead, it's important that you manage your image and reputation very carefully. Basically if you follow the one golden rule you'll be okay ...

Perhaps it's unfair to judge and compare the man at work with the man at home: but fair or unfair, that's just how it is. **Treat others exactly how you would like to be treated and add a sprinkle of 'extra' to go.**

One of the most interesting phenomena of the late Twentieth Century and the Twenty-first Century is the access to private and public information. We are a culture obsessed with gossip and private lives, private history and private motivation. Our compulsion to expose the 'real' man behind the empire or the 'real' woman behind the PR façade is sadly all too prolific. We have webcams, spycams, Big Brother TV shows and reality television. Then there are the endless exposé documentaries, replete with psychological profiles, 'expert' opinions and speculation.

As more and more of the world's population plugs into the World Wide Web and the information superhighway, and we become increasingly exposed, we have to be more vigilant about our integrity and image. This is especially true of business.

I don't want to encourage scare tactics or paranoia, yet I feel that often this topic is never mentioned in business books. It's almost taboo. Yet some of the fastest selling books are the *rise and fall stories*. There are too many examples of careers being interrupted or destroyed because of bad timing, poor choices and stupid or reckless indiscretions. We are all human, and sure we all make mistakes. But some mistakes are forgotten with a self-responsible clean up but unfortunately some mistakes just leave a permanent stain.

Business owners have to act a little like aeroplane pilots. There is a protocol about how and when to reveal *possible* bad news versus *definite* bad news ahead to your passengers and crew. Part of the pilot's job is to avert speculation and ultimately avoid panic.

As a business owner you have a duty and responsibility to only share issues with those with the responsibility and power to affect changes. There's little point in telling the 16-year-old trainee about financial burdens. Keeping morale high and your team focused on their designated task at hand is the priority. You face them with a smile. You can reserve your furrowed brow for your bookkeeper or accountant.

Often problems are solved way before they run away into a major crisis. But the rumour mill can take a lot longer to come to a standstill and can cause untold subtle damage. Self-containment is one of the key aspects of pristine management. I tried to have what I called the *I'm Loving It* face on most of the time.

Often as businesses expand and the staff under your guidance and supervision increase, you will have more and more eyes upon you. Some will just be waiting for you to fall. And yet in my experience, most of them are looking to you as role model. They are looking for clear mentorship and in many cases with the younger trainees, a trusted boss to shine a guiding light and strong direction; to be a pillar of potential.

I have to say that this was one of the most satisfying aspects of my job: to have had the mentorship and steering on an adventure course and then the opportunity to offer this back to all the trainees and staff under my management. I learned early on that to set an impeccable example was the best thing that I could do for myself and for my business. It was the ticket to securing a wonderfully stimulating and rewarding future.

Key Points

- Be discerning about the constructive and negative criticism you receive.

- Keep your nose clean and stay out of mischief.

- Take pride in your appearance and behaviour.

- Be appropriate and self contained with sensitive information.

- Be a pillar of potential for young eyes.

- Prove daily that you are trustworthy and deserving of respect.

- Lead by example.

- Dance like no one's watching and do business like everyone is watching.

Dance like no one's watching and do business like everyone is watching.

CHAPTER
21

SELF-RESPONSIBILITY FIRST

I'm being whimsical here but in all truth I learned early on that my first responsibility is to myself. I have a responsibility to my body, mind and spirit to be at my optimum. Everything else comes second. I learned that a healthy body really does support a sharper mind and a happier disposition.

I never liked the concept of getting the right *'balance'*. If you've worked for yourself for long enough you'll know that the balance tips weekly and sometimes daily. Perhaps it's semantics, but a word that works better for me is **harmony**. I could do various things in my

In the office I believe in doing my best, being authentic and being true to my word – at home I do my best, I am authentic and I am true to my wife's word.

business life, family life and personal life that invariably would look different each week and change ratio – but as long as they played some sort of harmonious chord, I knew I was on the right track. In short, I did my best to follow a regime and I remained flexible enough to keep the pressure of *'having to do it'* at bay.

**Opening of the Ronald McDonald Family room in Fiji.
Far right McDonald's Fiji Partner Marc McElrath.**

**Left to right
Craig McElrath Partner Fiji, Ronald McDonald, Maika and Natasha McElrath.**

Expanding and growing a business is a stressful process. It takes an extra concerted effort to keep a healthy mind and body to complete the task with your sanity in good working order, not to mention your heart and liver. I made personal fitness a hobby. I also used this time to reflect on all that I do have and have achieved as well as time to refashion my goals and life-path.

By keeping my core business values in the front of my mind I was able to get motivated. By keeping my goals and my values aligned I was able to stay motivated. When I worked hard and played hard I found I was able to spend much more quality time with my family.

Key points

- Make healthier choices for your body – it's the machine that needs daily servicing. Most people spend much more money on their car!

- Get interested in the science of health, read health magazines and stay inspired and focused within your new hobby.

- If you have time, take the stairs.

- A healthier you, leads to a healthier business.

- Illness always costs much more than you think.

> Make healthier choices for your body – it's the machine that needs daily servicing. Most people spend much more money on their car!

- Cultivate discipline, willpower, resilience and stamina.

CHAPTER
22

FULL CIRCLE

This is the shortest chapter and the most important. It's about your business plan. Remember we mentioned it in the beginning? What I did not mention is that your business plan is not linear. It has a beginning yes, but it has no fixed middle and certainly no end.

You should hear your business plan breathing in your briefcase or jumping up and down on your desk. It should be a living document that insists on being updated and considered daily. This should be a daily track record of vision versus reality. Scribble all over it, prove yourself right and prove yourself happily wrong. Update and re-evaluate, add new ideas and new technologies as they come your way.

Money and lifestyle illustrate either your very good luck or your hard earned accomplishments. Sometimes both.

So often during expansion you are expected to know so much about your business and the comprehensive business plan will have everything you need to know at the tip of your fingers. It's your business bible that will give you faith, and others will have faith in you. That, pretty much, is the secret dynamic of a healthy expanding business. You have faith in your product or service and the customer does too!

Traditional welcome in Fiji for the Leadership team from Australia.

CHAPTER
23

SUCCESS – IT MATTERS!

In 2001 I won the President's Award; the highest and most prestigious award in the McDonald's Empire. I had worked exceptionally hard and sales and profits reflected this. The award is given annually to the number one performer in a particular region or country. I received a substantial financial bonus and my wife and I were flown to the US for an amazing gala evening.

Two years prior to actually getting the award, I would fantasise about my winner's speech. What would I say and who would I thank? When I finally did give the speech, I was very well prepared. I knew exactly who to thank and knew without question that I was merely the conductor of an amazing orchestra. Yes, it's an important and skilled role but without a diligent and remarkable team I could not shine. I also knew that my training and support from the larger holding company was impeccable.

I once heard that success is quiet. I never really understood what that meant. I expected the noise of validation and appreciation to be deafening. I imagined, dreamed and daydreamed (all healthy pre-occupations) that it would feel loud and big. That somehow the intensity of the energy that leads to success, all the energy I had put in, would be somehow reflected back in one large supersonic bang.

Yes there was some noise but that was the noise of other people's ideas of success. After the accolades, awards, celebration and congratulatory mayhem there comes a time, usually just before you slide into sleep, when the 'quiet' comes in. It feels humble and soft. It actually feels like a deep appreciation and gratitude for the simple things.

Opening day of McDonald's in American Samoa.

Of course I was grateful for the money and the lifestyle but that's not what came to the fore. I could only think about my good health, my wife, my children, the good times, holidays, good colleagues, good friends etc. The culmination of years of dogged determination and hard yakka, have given me, and so many people around me, so much joy and aliveness. (I've been in Australia 23 years, so I've earned the right to use that very Australian term for work!)

Success for me is like a magnifying glass for all the ordinary things that I often would not or could not see or appreciate. The quiet of success put things into crystal-clear perspective for me.

When I parted with McDonald's in 2010, it was quite radical for my sense of identity and my habitual nature. In some ways I was in shock. I went from up to 100 emails a day to none. My diary was suddenly blank. Many of my social needs were met with my daily interactions with colleagues. Many of my friends were indeed colleagues. I felt a huge loss in my life and as though I'd been pushed into a dark hole.

Within a short time I began to remember the gifts that success had illuminated for me on the night of winning the President's Award. The quiet gift of gratitude for all that was deeply important to me. And when I emerged from this brief identity and existential crisis, I realised that all the beauty and joy in my life had not been made redundant. My job title had disappeared but my loving family, friends and my integrity were still present and shining. I learned a valuable lesson. I do my job but I am not my job.

To me there is only one real success story. That of any human being who realises and honours values that are beyond a certain kind of measure: values of love and friendship, loyalty and dignity and humble determination to do their best in all that they pursue. This understanding of success is energising and motivating.

When you bring this energy to your business, **everything is possible!!**

Key Points

- Always remember that you are one in an interconnected world both at home and in the workplace.

- Life, by its very nature, is teamwork.

- You do your job. You are not your job.

- The only constant is change. When change knocks you off your horse be very kind to yourself whilst jumping right back on.

- When radical change comes, welcome it and say out loud 'Hello opportunity!'

- Share everything you have and give back.

- Learn compassion, forgiveness and deeper understanding.

- Value your self and your contribution to life – it matters!

> You do your job. You are not your job.

LAST WORD

I thought that my Last Word for the book might be something like, *'I'm still loving it.'* But somewhere I think that's been well and truly established. It feels more heartfelt and true for me to simply say: 'Thank you'.

A big thank you to life; to opportunities; to success and failure equally; to time and distance that gives perspective that in turn evolves into wisdom; to my amazing good fortune; to my good health that affords me stamina, tenacity and ambition and to my desire to share and connect with my fellow travellers in this kaleidoscope we call life.

A big thank-you to Ray Kroc's tenacity and wisdom. Thanks to McDonalds, I have so far had a fantastic life, supersized and with fries!

Thanks to everyone who has contributed to my journey thus far and I look forward to all the friends that I have yet to meet.

Merrill Pereyra
www.expandyourbrand.com.au

LAST LAST WORD

"For when the One Great Scorer comes to mark against your name, He writes–not that you won or lost–but how you played the game." - Grantland Rice

Expand Your Brand